When twenty-five-year-old Greg flung himself in front of a speeding train in San Diego, devastated family and friends struggled for explanations. Why would a gifted, selfless person, with a winning sense of humor, end a promising future that began as a valued staffer at a distinguished Christian college? Unknown to all, beneath Greg's mask of cheerfulness hid a lifelong battle with personal significance. His diaries revealed the clues: *I'm unwanted . . . I'm lonely now . . . I will never be able to keep a job . . . Lord, help me!* His anguished cry expressed, "Lord I feel so small!"

And his cry mirrored my own.

Are these expressions isolated? No. A significant number of adults and teens fight a daily struggle to discover their place under the sun. The world's false yardsticks downgrade their worth. Feelings of insignificance overwhelm them. Daily battles with giants of fear, rejection, and comparison drain them. Lies hold them in bondage, aided by an enemy who deceives them of their true worth. The world, their families, and they themselves are robbed of their giftedness.

Is it possible to travel from the tortured lies of smallness to a sunrise of rock-solid confidence in God?

With God's help, our cries of anguish can be turned into shouts of victory.

LORD
I FEEL
SO SMALL

LORD
I FEEL
SO SMALL

USING GOD'S YARDSTICK TO CONQUER SELF-DOUBT

JON
DRURY

WinePressPublishing
Your Book, Defined. Since 1991.

WinePress Publishing (PO Box 428, Enumclaw, WA 98022) functions only as book publisher. As such, the ultimate design, content, editorial accuracy, and views expressed or implied in this work are those of the author.

ISBN 13: 978-1-4141-1804-8
ISBN 10: 1-4141-1804-X
Library of Congress Catalog Card Number: 2010906017

To Beverly, my wife, love and greatest friend,
and most insightful counselor, and to all those who hurt,
grasping for truth and God.

CONTENT

THANKS

WRITING TO CHANGE lives is more than an isolated endeavor. Special thanks to Karen O'Connor for her invaluable work on the manuscript. Thanks to the Hayward Writers Group, Susy Flory, Dianne Smith, Kari West, Carol Hall, and Gayle Gutierrez, for their professional edits and encouragement. The encouragement of the Castro Valley Christian Writers, the inspiration from the Christian Writers Seminar, and timely instruction from the Mt. Hermon Christian Writers Seminar were all invaluable. The forum of Vista, where many of the chapters appeared as articles, was invaluable in shaping these truths for communication. Thanks to Julie Gwinn of Broadman & Holman, Kim Bangs of Regal Publishing, and Rick Steele of AMG Publishers for their time and verbal encouragement. Thanks to Les Stobbe, agent and encourager, who believed in the manuscript and the need for this message.

You are invited to visit Jon on the web at http://www.jondrury.com. Additional resources related to *Lord I Feel So Small!* can be found there, including a more complete set of study questions that may be useful for a study group on significance.

or at his blog http://www.lordifeelsosmall.wordpress.com

PREFACE

WAS FEELIN' pretty small!" said my friend, Ken, at a vulnerable moment in his life. The statement clung to my memory because it crystallized my own lifelong battle with significance. As a Christian, I was supposed to know and live the answers. At times I would glance at my Bible, a red one with my name on the cover. I knew that it had all of God's answers. I just couldn't figure any of them out. My spirit cried, *Lord I feel so small!*

Since childhood, I have desperately sought to find my place under the sun, my unique contribution to the planet. We are all launched into this puzzling maze called life, and find it complicated by a variety of dead ends, clues, and periodic progress. How can we fulfill the powerful, unique call that the Lord has on our lives unless we know what it is? God Himself longs for the children He has begotten to know Him, know His plan, and make a powerful impact in the world around us. He longs for us to find the fulfillment every parent wants for their child.

No doubt for some finding significance is an easy pursuit. Perhaps just do what dad did. For me it was a huge, humiliating mystery, haunted by the shrieks of the other voice: *You are nothing.*

You are a loser and always will be. Your life is not significant. It is trash. Others may find their place, but you will never find yours. You are just a dust ball blowing around on the planet for a little while, of no importance to anyone. Though others may have a place, you have none and you never will have.

In my quest to find my place, the world's false yardsticks demeaned and devastated me. Daily I battled giants such as despair, fear, rejection, and comparison. For decades I studied the pages of Scripture, as a Christian, pastor, and counselor, but could not solve the puzzle. Often I had answers for others, but inside I traversed a dark tunnel, with very little light of day.

One day, in a rare moment of clarity, I stopped the car and scribbled on a scrap of paper all the things I believed about myself. I was a failure, desperately small in the human scheme of things. My scrawled notes shocked me. I saw that though deeply felt, compared with what I knew of God's love and purpose, they were all lies. Yet they clung to me like a dark cloud I could not rise above.

Are there answers? In the daily turmoil of emotions, conflicts, and doubts, it may seem there are no answers, and the only option is living confusion. It may seem that God is withholding the clues we desperately need. I concluded the answers were there, but my own confusion had blocked the channel of communication.

I was the problem.

Inwardly, and gradually through my suffering, a purpose grew that if I found the answers, I would attempt to follow them. It had to be an improvement on my daily agony. I do not think the determination came initially, but gradually as I agonized through the turmoil of daily existence. I longed to find my place under God.

Slowly, out of my brokenness, perhaps every year or two, the Lord would enable me to resolve one of the desperate emotions I faced. And each successful resolution opened a new world of hope. In my realm of need each one was revolutionary and life-changing.

I found my answers in the Bible, given by God as His provision for fragile human beings. The answers became the basis of a whole new realm of living.

When I had resolved a number of them, I had a growing desire to see others healed as I had been healed. I published an article entitled "Significant to God," summarizing my struggle and God's powerful answers. Larry, a friend who experienced similar conflicts, read the article. He commented, "This article is so helpful, I am going to read it every day."

Could the story of my desperate struggle and God's solutions be helpful in book form for a wider audience? What I have written records my sixty-year emotional struggle; my hope is the book will be of great help to others. I do not claim that my answers are new, previously unknown, or profound. But they were life-changing.

Why deal so deeply with human weakness? Why expose my own humiliating flaws? A student at a recent workshop I led found it incomprehensible that a pastor could struggle in these arenas. All of us grapple with daunting challenges in our humanity. Depicted here is my journey. My purpose is to help free others to find their joy and fulfillment in Christ, and that God be glorified.

The Bible? To my surprise, the answers to God's call and His plans for a human life, were and are all there, readable, and comprehensible. God longs for each of His beloved children to know them.

I invite you to journey with me as we discover together, and walk into a new sunrise of hope, fulfillment, and joy. *"Lord, I Feel So Small!"* moves from our agonized cry of smallness to explore twenty battlegrounds of significance. It seeks to expose the lies that demean, discover the miracle of God's purpose, and equip us for a life of unshakeable confidence.

CRAFTING THE FOUNDATION

CHAPTER 1

"LORD I FEEL SO SMALL!"

WHEN TWENTY-FIVE-YEAR-OLD GREG flung himself in front of a speeding train in San Diego, devastated family and friends struggled for explanations. Why would a gifted, selfless person, with a winning sense of humor, end a promising future that began as a valued staffer at a distinguished Christian college? Of medium height, with dark hair, Greg loved gatherings with others, including my children, and we loved having him in our home. After college, it was no surprise he took a staff position with Point Loma Nazarene.

Greg's diaries and letters revealed the clues. Beneath his mask of cheerfulness hid a lifelong battle with significance. In diary entries he cries *I'm unwanted . . . I'm lonely now . . . I will never be able to keep a job . . . Lord, help me!*

THE LYING VOICES

Is Greg's cry isolated? No. A significant number of adults and teens fight a daily struggle to discover their place under the sun. Those of us who have faced the battle know it well. We often cry, "Lord, I feel so small!" I know the daily emotional struggle, because for decades I viewed myself as a failure. Sadness overshadowed my life like a rain cloud on a sunny day; it was simply too obvious to ignore. Daily I could see little beyond a dark tunnel of hopelessness. In a crisis seven years ago, it seemed I could not go on. I thought the only thing I could do to benefit others was to give blood. I have given over fourteen gallons.

> For decades I viewed myself as a failure. Sadness, like a cloud, overshadowed my life.

For those who know me now, this will seem strange in the extreme. I am a former Air Force pilot, I have a master's degree, have pastored for thirty-three years, and am considered very successful by most. But I lived in constant slavery to this sense of smallness. Voices within echoed, *You're a failure. You will always be a failure. You lack the gifts and strengths of others. You are a small person, unworthy of love, and have no role or place on the planet.* Tragically they drowned out the high call of God.

Do these voices sound familiar? Only those of us engaged in this personal, bloody combat for our worth know the daily, moment-by-moment anguish that sometimes takes a life. More often it saps us of joy and fulfillment, and sentences us to wage a lifelong warfare to find our role in life.

How is it possible that a person would accept a verdict that placed him far below the place of honor and uniqueness God has for him? Why would he believe the lies? What is the true picture of one's significance?

One Fellow Struggler

For those of us that struggle, we are not alone. Elijah, the prophet of Israel, faced the same battle in 1 Kings 19. If you are not familiar with the Bible, stick with me. I think you will understand where I am going, and will find the prophet one with whom you can identify.

After years of powerful leadership as a prophet, fear gripped Elijah, and he ran for his life when threatened by Jezebel the vindictive queen. When he came to Beersheba in Judah, he left his servant, abandoning needed companionship, and fled into the desert. He came upon a juniper tree, sat down, and prayed that he might die. Listen to his self-deprecating words: "'I have had enough, LORD,' he said. 'Take my life; I am no better than my ancestors.' Then he lay down under the tree and fell asleep" (1 Kings 19:3-5).

Why would a powerful prophet cut and run after his greatest victory, the confrontation at Mt. Carmel? Following the dramatic firefall, the people cried, "The Lord He is God," (1 Kings 18:39). He could only conclude that his nation had finally come to faith in God. Afterwards, threatened by Jezebel, I believe he realized the acknowledgment of God he heard from the people was only a sham. Conditions would continue much as they had been with an idolatrous king and queen ruling a godless nation. The death of his lifelong dream crushed him, and he yielded to despair, considering himself a failure. He said, "I quit!"

> "I have had enough, LORD," he said. "Take my life...."

I Can't Go On!

Just as Elijah faced his crisis, I faced one in June 1998. During a vacation in Yosemite National Park, I received distressed calls from my church that areas of my ministry were falling apart. It reinforced the lies within, and already emotionally depleted, I felt I could not go on. This crisis was nothing new. I was frequently at the end of my resources, yet always seemed to persevere, despite pain and desperation.

I cried out to God in my inward darkness. In the coming weeks, the Lord began not only bringing light, but also to diagnose the root problems that had chained me most of my life. I started with the book *Search for Significance* by Robert S. McGee. At a point of great need, I grabbed the book like a drowning man. Unexpectedly, each sentence of diagnosis and cure was a burning sword plunged into my heart. I found every sentence painful as it revealed the code of lies I had lived by.

> Why would a person accept a verdict that places him far below the high place that God has for him?

I also found that those deceptions about my place in life had given birth to individual battleground issues such as despair, fear, and worry. In the pages ahead, I will take you to these areas. They may be the same ones you face.

These areas represent lies about God and us. But the central lie that empowers all the others is unbelief in God, who He is, what He has said, and what He has revealed about the human race He has created. The individual lies are symptoms, but unbelief is the real disease.

In contrast, God details our significance as exemplified in Luke 15. The religious leaders, angered that Christ was associating with people they considered unholy, grumbled among themselves that He received sinners and ate with them. Their hatred toward Him could be cut with a knife. The practice of the religious leaders was to disdain association with such people and display a false mask of holiness.

Christ tells three stories that illustrate how each person He created is priceless; the religious leaders had missed learning the infinite value of one person. It is interesting that the despised tax collectors and sinners were freely coming to Christ. They were drawn by His love and esteem for them.

You're Insignificant!

The world says: *You're just one in six billion, of no importance to anyone!*

To these leaders of the Jewish faith, Jesus answered their accusation by asking a question about a single lost sheep (Luke 15:1-7). One sheep out of a flock of one hundred is missing. Someone might say, "Why bother? It's only a 1 percent loss. Forget about it!" But Christ and His hearers knew that in their pastoral society, the shepherd would go to great lengths to seek even one that was lost. When found, it would be tenderly cared for (the animal may have been injured), and the subject of rejoicing.

> Not only do the Father and I receive sinners, each one is valued beyond measure.

Jesus' story reproved the religious leaders, who were not only willing that the majority be devalued, but also actively drove them away as unworthy. They based their evaluation on a flawed judgment that the common people were rebels against God, unworthy of His care. They missed the truth that God seeks all, even rebels and self-righteous religious leaders.

Christ answers their attitude and actions: *You are right. Not only do the Father and I receive sinners, each one is valued beyond measure. They are so prized by me that I give myself to seek and save each one!*

You're Worthless!

Another lie is: *You're worthless! You have no value as a person!*

Having asked what a shepherd would commonly do, He now asks what a woman would do. In Luke 15:8-10, Christ describes a woman who had lost one out of ten coins of her bridal headdress, a gift at her betrothal. For many poor brides of the East, it would have been their most precious possession.

The coins were drachmas, about the same value as a Roman denarius or a day's wage. The loss paralleled losing a diamond in a diamond ring. Searching quickly became imperative; with a dirt floor it would quickly become discolored, disfigured, and harder to find. It might be stepped on repeatedly and eventually become buried.

Notice the extreme personal effort. The search would not be abandoned until the precious coin was found.

When my parents were newly married, at a time of need they pawned my mother's engagement ring as they traveled across country. We kids always asked, "Why didn't you go back and get the ring?" Sadly, they never made it a priority.

Christ seeks each of us and longs to rescue us and buy us back through His extreme personal effort—His death on the cross. In His work, He shows His evaluation of each of us: you are unique and priceless to Me!

You're Unworthy!

Perhaps the most damaging evaluation is *I have failed. I am unworthy of forgiveness.*

Luke 15:11-32 tells the story of a young son who asked his father for his share of the inheritance while his father was still alive. His selfish request brought dishonor to his father. Despite the insult, the compassionate father released his son, no doubt with the prayer that he would eventually become a repentant and mature individual.

How far did the son fall? He lived loosely, ruining his reputation, morals, and finances, and dishonored his heritage and his God. The son's fall was complete. But at the bottom of his fortunes he came to his senses—the very thing for which the father (and probably the unmentioned mother) prayed.

Bible scholars say that a similar story was told in Jewish society, with a different twist. When the son returned and said, "I am no longer worthy to be called your son." the father answers, "I have no son!" and in essence, slams the door in his face.

Christ knew the story and changed the ending to reflect the boundless love of the Father. He showed that unworthy, unde-serving people can change and be embraced with rejoicing. *You reject sinners because of their sin. I seek sinners! In their failure is eligibility for my rescue. I change the unworthy into honored members of my own family.*

> You reject sinners because of their sin. I seek sinners!

FINDING TRUE GREATNESS

Truths such as these have proven life-changing for me. I find I must immerse myself, swim in, and breathe them continually to combat the world of lies within and outside of me.

It has not been a short journey; painful battles have to be fought daily, and new truths assimilated into my mindset. However, it has been the most profitable journey of my life since coming to faith in Christ. For me, the answer has enabled my daily thought processes to begin moving from sadness to joy.

My friend, Greg, who took his own life, left heart-wrenching journals that belied his struggle. As I read them and listened to the testimonials at his memorial service, I was overcome by tears. Over and over in Greg's notes, the false conclusion he reached was, *What a failure I am!* My conclusion differed. I concluded he had missed his own greatness. He couldn't see what others saw and thought he was nothing. He failed to see he was the touch of God in countless lives around him.

> Are you missing
> the picture of your
> true greatness?

Are you missing the picture of your true greatness? Have you ever caught a glimpse of that picture? You may not be beside the railroad tracks of decision, but nonetheless facing a desperate daily struggle. If so, I have walked in your shoes.

As we journey perhaps we can learn together. We can begin to defuse the lies that are killing us, and find the significance and greatness God intended for each of us.

Think It Through

1. Why do so many people struggle with feelings of smallness?

2. What lies about your own significance have you harbored?

3. How are these lies about our own place really unbelief in God?

4. How did Christ's version of the story of the prodigal and his father differ from the one told in Jewish society?

5. How do the lies we tell ourselves cause us to miss our greatness? Who is shortchanged in the process?

CHAPTER 2

FOUNDATIONS FOR SIGNIFICANCE

JUDY'S PARENTS INITIATED the lies and rejection she battled through much of her life. "You're not as pretty as your sister," her dad would say, then hug his favorite. Her mother also referred to her children with profanity, emphasizing they were unwanted. After Judy married, her parents disowned her, even taking the pillow she had slept on. The rejection of her childhood fostered an abysmally poor image of herself. Perhaps there were similar negative elements in your own family.

> You're not as pretty as your sister!

IRREPLACEABLE FOUNDATION

God has designed the family unit as the core foundation not only for society, but for determining our own significance (Deuteronomy 4:9; 6:4-9; 11:18-21; Psalm 78:1-8). These passages reflect God's plan for the continuous dedication of parents to their children, not only by communicating spiritual values, but by bestowing individual time and nurture. When we fulfill these biblical models, children receive a deep reservoir of resources and confidence to find their place. They are prepared not only to be stable, mature adults, but often to be leaders and models who powerfully affect others. The converse is also true as rejection, conditional acceptance, or a lack of nurture leave a fractured foundation.

> I wondered . . . why my mom didn't value me enough to be home for me.

Why would a parent fail to impart encouragement to his or her own child? Obviously all parents are flawed to some degree. They may have seen poor role models throughout their childhood, and in turn reflect what they've learned. They may fail to perceive the crucial lifelong impact of the home. Some parents are immature, ill-equipped, or unwilling to embrace the selflessness needed for parenting. For many, the child is only a frustrating interruption of their own lives.

BUILDING BLOCKS

The crucial building blocks for a child's proper, biblical sense of worth must be laid by his parents or guardians.

Time—time spent with the child. It has been said that love is spelled t-i-m-e. I remember my three siblings and me around my mother's ironing board when we were small. As she ironed, she told stories of Little Joe, a pilot who had his own airplane, and flew like Sky King of 50s television fame. Perhaps the images contributed to my own service later as a U.S. Air Force pilot.

Beth, a homemaker and writer, says of her mother, " . . . she did not stay home and raise me . . . she always worked outside the home . . . we were shuffled from babysitter to babysitter . . . I wondered what made my friend, Sandy, so special that her mother stayed home to raise her, and why my mom didn't value me enough to be home for me."

Granted, with the economics of life, both parents—or the single parent—often have to work, but time must be found for one-on-one nurture.

Affection—My father was physically affectionate and would kiss the four of us. He would not do so in public to avoid embarrassing us, but in our own home he always showed fondness. As a guy, I had to pretend to hate it: "Dad, no. Don't kiss me!" It made no difference; he kissed me anyway, and it was one of the strongest evidences that I was loved and valued by my parents. Physical affection has great power to communicate value.

I always felt it was important as a dad to be physically affectionate toward my daughters, within bounds. My purpose was not only to communicate love, but also to prepare them to be affectionate with their own husbands and children. My affection toward my son took the form of wrestling, playing, or competing in sports together.

> My aunt's words of affirmation played over in my mind and became the promise of things to come.

Affirming Words—In childhood I had an eccentric aunt who lived in an idyllic home surrounded by oak trees. As a young boy of six or seven she would say to me, "Someday God is going to do something great with you." She repeated the statement periodically when I would see her and I never forgot her words. She believed in me. Through the next decade of schooling, though I felt invisible to those around me, was a poor student, and clumsy at sports, my aunt's affirmation played over in my mind and became the promise of things to come.

When Beth said to her father, "Hey, Dad; guess what?" He answered "Let's see, you ran away and nobody cared?" She came to hate those thoughtless words, which raised questions about her value as a person.

Parental Character/Consistency—A parental model of character is a powerful influence. In my own home, though my dad was an affectionate father, he battled with mental health and seldom worked. He smoked two or three packs a day, and lacked the discipline and stability to hold a job. He periodically became captivated by various hobbies and interests, at one point organizing reunions for his Iowa college. I never saw him model a work ethic that carried difficult projects through to completion. He always took the easy route.

Where my dad lacked, my mother more than made up. She was the sole financial support of our family, was loving, hardworking, and consistent.

Discipline—The purpose of discipline in parenting is to develop self discipline throughout life. Perhaps in decades past, strict parental discipline was the norm, but the pattern emerging today is one of parents who fail to discipline their children. They may lack the conviction and firmness to impress upon their children the lessons that are vital for life. Often I see homes where a child is indulged, spoiled, and idolized. I have noted this produces directionless, self-centered, undisciplined adults, and sometimes prison inmates. The purpose of discipline is to point the child to the best values. One of my daughters commented about parenting in our home: "My parents used discipline as a teaching tool more than a punishment."

Yes, in many homes there is a danger of overbearing discipline. One of my friends said, "The only time I saw my dad was when he beat me." How much discipline is enough? I suggest using the minimum necessary force to reinforce loving nurture.

Loving Marriage—Someone has said, "The most important thing you can do for your children is love your spouse." Though it may seem an intangible, it is a powerful force in communicating security to the child, and nurturing a proper sense of significance. Reflecting on her parents, one of my daughters noted, "There was a loving relationship that existed between my mom and my dad."

> Mom and Dad fought at night . . . I heard every word. My security hung by a thread . . .

My own parents had moments when they fought over finances because my father was poor at handling money. He often purchased on whims, and bills went unpaid, twice causing bankruptcy.

Mom and Dad fought at night after we children had gone to bed, and I heard every word. My security hung by a thread as I concluded that our home would break up in the morning. We remained together, but the cloud of insecurity followed me into adulthood.

Spiritual Nurture—A current mindset is, "I'll let my children choose their religion." This is abdication of the responsibility to point our children to God. My mom possessed a strong Christian faith and purposed to nurture us in that faith. She led us in memorizing Scripture at the meal table, which in our home was a picnic table, the only dining table we could afford. My sisters excelled while I was a slow student. Mom took us to the First Presbyterian Church even when I resisted. She led me through the prayer of faith when I was seven, and her own life of prayer was a model for her family.

The Scriptures point to nurture that is a continual meaningful contact between parent and child:

"These commandments that I give you today are to be upon your hearts. Impress them on your children. Talk about them when you sit at home and when you walk along the road, when you lie down and when you get up" (Deuteronomy 6:6-7).

Timely Release—As your children approach the teenage years, aim toward gradually releasing them into adulthood. Allow more responsibility and freedom. If they fail some of the tests, loving correction and discipline must intervene. As a parent, be committed to their eventual release, or you will stunt their maturing to adulthood. You may produce an overly dependant adult or one angry at your inability to let go.

I always loved teaching my teens to drive. As they approached the legal age, they naturally wanted to get their driver's license. I had my system, starting in the school parking lot, teaching them how to use the stick shift, brake, and accelerator. We then took simple trips around the block, graduated to city streets, and finally navigated freeway traffic. They learned all the skills necessary for safe and defensive driving. My time with them also showed that I was committed to their adulthood and freedom.

> God longs to fulfill infinitely all you lacked in your own home.

"I HAD NONE OF THIS!"

After reading this list of building blocks, your response may be, "I had none of this; I never had this foundation!" In fact the list may have been painful to review. Let me suggest four things.

Immerse Yourself in God's Love. First John 3:1 says to those who have come to faith in Christ, "How great is the love the Father has lavished on us, that we should be called children of God!" (1 John 3:1a). Romans 8:37-39 says nothing can separate us from the love of God. Study God's love in the Scriptures, meditate on it, swim in it. If you have longed for love because of the emptiness in your own background, revel in God's love.

Enter God's Family. By faith in Christ, accept the Heavenly Father as your divine parent. John 1:12 declares, "Yet to all who received him, to those who believed in his name, he gave the right to become children of God" (John 1:12). Those who in repentance and faith come to Him, are welcomed as children into God's family (Appendix 1). The new family relationship is crucial to show the believer's loving relationship to his Lord and to other members of the family of faith.

Trust God as Your Perfect Parent. He longs to fulfill infinitely all you lacked in your own home. He proves His affection in what He gave for us:

"For you know that it was not with perishable things such as silver or gold that you were redeemed . . . but with the precious blood of Christ, a lamb without blemish or defect" (1 Peter 1:18-19).

He declares how precious we are to Him (Luke 12:6-7). He shows His love for His children by His presence: "And surely I am with you always, to the very end of the age" (Matthew 28:20b).

Be a Pioneer. In what you lacked in your own home, determine to be a pioneer. Though loving actions were not modeled before you, break new ground by living them out before your own family and those around you. I mentioned Beth above and her absent mother. Beth determined to be a pioneer, living out a new model before her own children and giving them adequate time by home schooling them.

Judy, the woman rejected by her father, was drawn to another Father. She said," When I received Christ, at around age thirty-five, I cried with joy for weeks. The scales fell off my eyes and I could see clearly who God really was. I felt like Paul at Damascus. I realized God was a loving God—He was a real Father to me . . . He accepted me the way I was."

She began to find her significance and opportunities opened to show the love of the Father. She ministered in choirs, sang solos, contributed in drama, and taught Sunday School. Though raised in a home of cruelty, rejection, and comparison, Judy now seeks, through God's grace, to pass on to her family a heritage of love and faith. Though she lacked godly nurture as a child, she is determined to forge a new way for her family. She now listens to the Father, who has rebuilt the foundation of her value as an individual: *You are precious and perfect in my sight. Believe in my high call on your life. Trust me and touch the world with my love!*

Think It Through

1. Why do some parents fail to impart the encouragement and nurture needed by a child?

2. On what basis can we say that the family is the foundation for significance?

3. How would you answer those who hold that the classroom, church, or "village" should impart the primary values to a child?

4. If you lacked a positive foundation, where do you start in rebuilding?

5. Is God's provision really powerful and significant enough to fill the gap?

CHAPTER 3

YARDSTICKS OF TRUE WORTH

T HE MAN STOOD over the newborn baby's bassinet. The proud mother drew back the blanket to reveal her treasure, then paused to listen to what the observer had to say. With an angry visage he spewed, "That's the most useless, ugly baby I have ever seen!"

FLAWED MEASURE

The above situation is imaginary. We would all howl with indignation at anyone saying such terrible words. However, many of us regularly apply that same faulty measure of worth to ourselves. Human beings measuring themselves by flawed standards spell disaster for both the measurer and the measured. It destroys finding our true worth in God.

I watched second-grader, Troy, drive for the basket. Skilled

> Human beings measuring themselves by flawed standards spells disaster.

for someone so young, he elevated for a lay-up from the right side of the basket. The ball hit the rim, then bounced away. No basket. I looked at his parents at that instant. Their expressions fell from hope to disappointment. He had failed them. He had made them failures. Their expressions showed rejection and anger.

The incident happened in my first experience coaching boys in an outdoor practice. Troy's parents were over-involved in the process. From their view it was all about them, not their son. The experience grieved me. I wanted to scream, "What are you doing? Is a basket worth more than a boy?"

WHO'S MEASURING?

For many in our society a basket is worth more than a boy. We evaluate people by goals, incomes, popularity, appearance, and success. Many have been devalued throughout their entire lives.

> I was a failure in their eyes.

As we saw with Judy in Chapter 2, families can measure the worth of a child with a flawed yardstick. "I questioned my significance because my parents didn't believe in me . . . I didn't do what they wanted. I was a failure in their eyes." Families often injure the ones they love—or are supposed to love. They measure by their own defective standard or compare family members to each other.

The world's yardstick is flawed. Avoid it.

In seminary, I took a course on graphics as an aid to communication. A young lady in the course said, "My husband and I drive a Porsche. All of our friends drive Porsches." Perhaps she intended to impress. She obviously felt a cut above the average because she drove a nicer car than most.

In Lloyd's battle with significance he notes ". . .we are in a performance-oriented society. For most people, we are only important to them as long as we can perform and meet their needs."

Buying Into the Standard

One tragic result of this measuring is that often we buy it. Beth came to believe, "I am what others think, feel, say, or believe that I am . . . I take the evaluations of others as truth . . ."

In Lynn's home, each member of her family was a star: her dad a Harvard grad, her mom the president of her nursing college, her brother a successful basketball player at 6' 8". Lynn felt like a nothing: too fat, unattractive, and lacking intelligence. Though the family never communicated this, Lynn was measuring herself.

A college girl logs hours in front of the mirror, angered that her appearance does not fulfill college ideals. She feels cheated by God, rejecting the real beauty and design He intended. When we compare we substitute shifting, flawed human standards for the perfect values of God. Self criticism on this basis is destructive.

Why do we take these flawed standards and measure ourselves by them? I hope this realization angers you. It does me. I have lived with the lies too long.

One Person's Measure

"I have been created inferior to others," I concluded in high school. I measured myself by the sports stars and leaders my school idolized. I was slow to develop, did poorly in class, and was inept at sports. The conclusion of being created inferior grieved me, because I had tender feelings for God. I did not know

I had concluded that my worth was determined by comparison.

why He loved me less, but it was obvious. When I measured my gifts, abilities, and achievements against those of others I came up short.

College had its own yardstick. I came to understand that the elite in the college scene were the "Greeks"—the fraternity and sorority members. Working my way through college, starting with junior college, I felt small without the big ring and big ego of a fraternity guy.

Even when serving as a pastor in my first church, a rural church with 100 members, I could not escape my own flawed measurement. When I attended pastoral conferences I wanted to crawl out the back door. I grieved, comparing myself with seemingly more gifted leaders, and my church with fellowships that were larger and had more successful programs.

In all of these arenas the real problem was not others evaluating me, but my evaluation of myself. I had written false values into my own consciousness. I had concluded that my worth was determined by comparison.

GRASSHOPPERS AND COMPARISON

When you compare what you seem to lack with what others seem to possess, intimidation replaces trust.

Consider the failure of the ten spies that examined the land of Canaan. In Numbers 13, God commanded twelve spies to view the land of Canaan, the land promised to them by God. They took forty days to examine the land and formulate their report. When they returned, ten of the spies brought a report of comparison:

But the men who had gone up with him said, "We can't attack those people; they are stronger than we are." And they spread among the Israelites a bad report about the land they had explored. "The land we explored devours those living in it. All the people we saw there are of great size. We saw the Nephilim there (the descendants of Anak come from the Nephilim). We seemed like grasshoppers in our own eyes, and we looked the same to them."

—Numbers 13:31-33

When you compare what you seem to lack with what others seem to possess, intimidation replaces trust. In this case, their intimidation led the whole nation to rebel against God's good provision of the land. They refused to enter, and God judged them with a forty-year wait, while the entire disobedient generation died. Comparison brought disaster.

Comparison brings disaster to our own lives as well. Attempting to live life apart from the foundation of truth—who we are under God—derails us from our true giftedness and call. The last thing we need is to be a clone of someone else, or rob someone of what we envy. Comparing ourselves to others is a great danger and can bring us to ruin.

The disobedient spies failed to consider what God said was unique about them. The God of the burning bush, the Red Sea deliverance, and the pillar of cloud and fire had called them to be victorious conquerors. They were different from all other peoples.

UNIQUENESS

The apostle Paul gives instruction about how people measure themselves:

We do not dare to classify or compare ourselves with some who commend themselves. When they measure themselves by themselves and compare themselves with themselves, they are not wise. We, however, will not boast beyond proper limits, but will confine our boasting to the field God has assigned to us, a field that reaches even to you.

—2 Corinthians 10:12-13

Notice his warning about measuring ourselves against others, and his focus on the area of giftedness and endeavor that God had assigned to each. This needs to be our focus, our unique place and call, and the instructions of the God who has called us. Consider a parallel passage of instruction:

If anyone thinks he is something when he is nothing, he deceives himself. Each one should test his own actions. Then he can take pride in himself, without comparing himself to somebody else, for each one should carry his own load.

—Galatians 6:3-5

I remember a wall being constructed as a barrier between the freeway and my neighborhood. At one point during construction, I could not believe my eyes. Some worker had mortared blocks that stood out from the flat surface of the wall. It angered me; taxpayers' money had been wasted. The offending blocks would have to be smashed and replaced. As the next few days passed, the wall continued to rise. More blocks stood out from the surface. I was puzzled. Finally the wall was complete. Then I realized the offending blocks were part of a pleasing pattern, a design repeated throughout the length of the wall, and now seen in many parts of our state.

We have all been angered or wounded because we did not measure up to others. Yet God has created each of us in a unique way.

True Measure and the Daily Struggle

How then should we measure ourselves? Let me share some conclusions. The first is that our highest goal should be to please God. We must constantly turn to God, not man, for His evaluation of us. Notice Paul's statement of that purpose: "So we make it our goal to please him, whether we are at home in the body or away from it" (2 Corinthians 5:9).

This fits with the purpose of the Savior, to always please the Father: "The one who sent me is with me; he has not left me alone, for I always do what pleases him" (John 8:29).

We must continually turn away from false human opinion, the measure of our families, society's defective gauge, and the devastating devaluation of ourselves by internal assessment. We must then place ourselves before our God, His holy character, and His Word. He is our standard, our measure, and through his Son, He has declared us as righteous in His sight.

But how can a human being ever please an infinite, holy God? It begins with personally coming to Christ in repentance and faith, and continues by growth in the faith, and a growing closeness to our Savior by developing our relationship with Him. It is not an easy path. We are engaged in spiritual warfare, and struggle will be part of our journey. It is written across the pages of Scripture and seen in the examples I have shared. Like the Israelites entering their promised land, you too may sometimes feel like a grasshopper in a land of giants.

Our Opportunity and Call

Pleasing God and faithfulness to Him in our unique call in life is depicted in a story told by the Savior.

A man leaving on a trip entrusted various amounts of his finances to servants in his employ. When he returned he said to one servant "Well done, good and faithful servant! You have been faithful with a few things; I will put you in charge of many things. Come and share your master's happiness!

—Matthew 25:21

While comparison emphasizes what is different about us, there is one thing that is the same about us. We all have the opportunity to trust the Master and obey Him. This faithfulness, and His approval, brings our highest sense of significance.

> We are just as precious to God as a newborn infant.

To the Lord whom we seek to please, we are as unique as a newborn baby. In a passage that speaks about the initiation of human life in the womb, God talks about the preciousness of each of us, and our value and significance before Him. In Psalm 139:1-18 He says, "You are not alone, I will never leave you" (verses 1-8); "I am leading you by my hand" (verses 9-12); "I designed you perfect according to my plan" (verses 13-16a); "I have designed your moments and your days" (verse 16b); "You are constantly on my mind" (verses 17-18).

The result: we revel in the fact that we are just as precious to God as a newborn infant. We must accept no other verdict, whether from family, the world, or ourselves.

Think It Through

1. How do we justify evaluating others by wrong measure?

2. What is the danger of destructive self-criticism?

3. How did comparison prove disastrous for the ten spies and the people? How is it disastrous for us?

4. How should we measure ourselves?

5. If God's approval is our chief goal, how do we start the process of pleasing him?

FEELINGS THAT IMMOBILIZE US

CHAPTER 4

TRANSFORMING DESPAIR INTO HOPE

L LOYD LOST HOPE. During his late twenties, he worked the night shift as a security guard while attempting to finish school during the day. He couldn't keep up with the frantic pace of life. "I guess I was mad at God for my position in life. I felt He had made a mistake and one day I thought about suicide. I wore a gun on my job so it would have been so easy. My wife found me distraught, lying on the grass in the back yard."

Lloyd despaired, believing he had failed himself, his family, and God.

THE DEATH OF HOPE

Despair is the loss of hope. We live in a society dominated by despair. It is the reason the homeless person has given up, the streetwalker has surrendered her character, and the husband and father has abandoned his marriage and family. Its danger lurks in every realm, regardless of our accomplishments.

I remember my own loss of hope as I ministered to eighty single men and women in my church. When we lost our singles pastor, they reeled, as his mature, caring leadership had built the group. They plummeted in spirit and attendance. Another pastor and I stepped in to give some stability, but nothing could stem the tide. Eventually the other pastor left, and my wife, Beverly, and I shouldered the load.

Despair is the loss of hope. Its danger lurks in every realm.

We threw ourselves into this ministry with all we had, teaching, leading, learning, and planning special events. We were full of dreams and anticipation when we began, but after two years of love and labor, the group was weaker than ever, and I could feel internal conflict brewing beneath the surface. In my growing despair, I blamed everybody, especially myself. "I have failed. If only I were more of a charismatic leader. I have failed my group, my church, and most of all my God!" I sought the back door as a way to bail out in some acceptable manner.

THE DISEASE OF DESPAIR

After my experience with the singles group, I taught a men's Bible study on obstacles that men face and finally grasped the stark reality of my battle with despair. Grappling with the Scriptures and the insights of Patrick Morley in *The Man in the Mirror*, I faced my struggle for the first time. I realized the disease was not only connected to my singles ministry, but had characterized many periods of my life.

The discovery of my despair startled me.

The discovery of my despair startled me. How did I get here? How does a person handle loss of hope in life and ministry, especially when facing impossible challenges? How can one turn around and find hope in God once again? How can the foundation be rebuilt, or can it? Just as He had during many other times of weakness, the Lord met me with real answers. He pointed me to a study in the Scriptures to shed light on my hopelessness, and to find God's cure. I trust my discoveries will be useful to you.

THOSE WHO DESPAIRED

Scripture gives many examples of despairing saints.

- Sarah longed for the child of promise and said to Abraham, "The LORD has kept me from having children. Go, sleep with my maidservant; perhaps I can build a family through her" (Genesis 16:2b).
- Jacob signaled hopelessness in his words to Pharaoh: "The years of my pilgrimage are a hundred and thirty. My years have been few and difficult, and they do not equal the years of the pilgrimage of my fathers" (Genesis 47:).
- When Naomi returned to Bethlehem after the death of her husband and both of her sons, she said, "'Don't call me Naomi (pleasantness),' she told them. 'Call me Mara (bitterness), because the Almighty has made my life very bitter'" (Ruth 1:20).

With our perfect hindsight we can see that, despite the loss of hope and desperate circumstance, God was still working in a powerful way for each of these distressed saints. He was still supremely worthy of their trust.

MEASURING HOPELESSNESS

As I examined the Scriptures, and my own experience, I made surprising discoveries.

- In many arenas of life I had measured myself by human standards alone, relying on my perception of how life should be and what I should accomplish. Rarely did I turn to God for His perspective.
- My hopes had been founded on my own expectations. Our dreams are a sensitive area for all of us, but human expectations not consecrated to God are a slam dunk for disappointment. We must make the Lord alone the God of our plans and our future.

> At the center of my hopelessness was a focus on 'self' . . . my dreams, my hopes, my plans, my feelings.

- At times I had placed my hope on material things. I remembered the car I idolized and financed on credit. I loved to look at it and drive it. Then the engine blew up and I grieved. The Lord allowed me to see this idol as a flawed basis of hope.
- I found that perhaps my greatest despair was with people. I remembered those who rejected me, failed me, or blocked my dreams. I harbored resentment against others who I perceived had injured or betrayed me. I seemed unwilling or unable to see they were not to blame. My problem was my attitude.
- At the center of my hopelessness I discovered a focus on *self*. I was addicted to *my* dreams, *my* hopes, *my* plans, *my* feelings. When I measured the causes of my hopelessness, I found myself at the center, instead of the Lord I said I served.

Never Give Up!

Another conclusion that clearly addressed my despair came from a story Jesus told:

> Then Jesus told his disciples a parable to show them that they should always pray and not give up. He said: "In a certain town there was a judge who neither feared God nor cared about men. And there was a widow in that town who kept coming to him with the plea, 'Grant me justice against my adversary.'"
>
> —Luke 18:1-3

God reminded His children to never give up. The context of the story of the widow and the judge shows the great resource we have in difficult circumstances. God provides us with the avenue of believing prayer, and He is a God who hears and answers our prayers.

Still my mind screamed. "Why? Where, then, do I turn? Do I keep hoping when the situation is hopeless? That seems insane!" I found the solution reflected in a dual experience of the apostle Paul.

> God reminded His children to never give up.

Dual Experience

Considering the opposition and trials they were facing, Paul evaluated the likelihood of survival. Using the Greek word translated despair, he concludes that they would probably lose their lives.

> We do not want you to be uninformed, brothers, about the hardships we suffered in the province of Asia. We were under great

pressure, far beyond our ability to endure, so that we despaired
even of life.

—2 Corinthians 1:8

But how does this tally with Luke 18:1 where Christ instructed
that we never lose hope? That is where Paul's other use of the
word comes in. A couple of chapters later in his book, he gives
the balancing factor:

> Paul *felt* human despair
> . . . *but* he never
> despaired of his hope
> and belief in Jesus Christ.

We are hard pressed on every
side, but not crushed; perplexed,
but not in despair; persecuted,
but not abandoned; struck
down, but not destroyed.

—2 Corinthians 4:8-9

How in one statement could he
say he despaired, and in another
say he refused to despair? The second reference has to do with his
hope in the Lord. Notice the context of his refusing to despair:

We always carry around in our body the death of Jesus, so that
the life of Jesus may also be revealed in our body. For we who
are alive are always being given over to death for Jesus' sake, so
that his life may be revealed in our mortal body.

—2 Corinthians 4:10-11

The great apostle could evaluate human circumstances realisti-
cally, and sometimes despair on planet Earth, *without despairing of
Christ.* Therein lies the answer. Paul *felt* human despair when he
saw sin and hopelessness all around him, *but* he never despaired
of his hope and belief in Jesus Christ.

HOPE IN GOD ALONE

Like Paul, my hope needed a different objective in all the puzzling, frustrating affairs of life. The model of Scripture showed the hope of God's children is to be fixed on Him alone.

> But now, Lord, what do I look for? My hope is in you.
> —Psalm 39:7

> Why are you downcast, O my soul? Why so disturbed within me? Put your hope in God, for I will yet praise him, my Savior and my God.
> —Psalm 42:5-6a

> For you have been my hope, O Sovereign LORD, my confidence since my youth.
> —Psalm 71:5

This was the missing piece of the puzzle. This was the solution for my despair. I need not live in a hopeless state, constantly grieved by dreams that had died. I needed to take the hope I had fixed on human expectations, and place it on God alone. Once I understood this, it brought me to a crossroads. Was I willing to forsake despair and the idolatry of my human dreams apart from God?

> I needed to take the hope I had fixed on human expectations, and place it on God alone.

I remember the moment I prayed, acknowledging to God that I was removing my expectation from everything in the human arena and placing it on Him. "Lord, I see it now. Forgive me for displacing You with my own goals and idols. I place my hope on You alone."

FRUITS OF HOPE IN GOD

During the next couple of days things began to change. I had prayed with no expectations, just trying to yield to the new truth I had discovered. What happened caught me unaware.

When I placed my hope on God alone, with no expectation of return, hope returned to me. Where I had been plagued by unbelief, doubt, and despair, my spiritual eyes began to open to God and what He could do. My faith began to grow.

Other steps of growth occurred when deep trials made their inevitable visit. However, instead of moving toward hopelessness, I began to forge a different path, looking to the Lord alone. Where I had felt trapped, with no way out, I now began to see possibilities. And because this path was a new one, I went slowly, one step at a time, following God's will and direction.

Other results were a deeper and more joyful walk with my Lord. I was beginning to see more of the life of victory God had intended for His children. I also experienced more confident living in the world of men. Instead of constantly being battered by doubts and fears, I finally had an anchor in God alone.

And as I continued to rest and trust in God for the impossible, I increasingly saw Him working the impossible on my behalf. And even when I didn't recognize progress, I knew God was in charge and all things would work together for good.

I saw that same dependence reflected in the life of one of my seminary professors, Dr. Dwight Pentecost. Before class on one occasion, he shared that his wife's health had improved. One of the students commented "Isn't God good!"

Dr. Pentecost replied, "Yes, God is good. But be careful. God is good whether she improves or not!"

Our hope is in God alone. And ours must not be a fair weather faith, only trusting when things work to our outward advantage. God is working on our behalf even through great trials and heartbreak.

Hope and Significance

I began the chapter with the story of Lloyd's despair, and desire to end his life. After finding God's solution Lloyd said, "Suicide would have been easy, but two things helped. I knew I would be letting God and Pamela (my wife) down, and I knew God loved me and cared for me. I finally realized I was exactly who God wanted me to be and I was where He wanted me. I kept the same job, but when I saw my job as my ministry, life took on significance."

Because of God and His promises, though we may despair of human circumstances, we live in constant hope in our faithful Heavenly Father, who delivers us and works His victorious will through us.

Think It Through

1. When have you, like Lloyd, battled despair? What inward conclusions brought you to that place?

2. What evidence do you see that some are dominated by despair?

3. Read Ruth 1. Despite Naomi's justifiable sorrow, what incorrect conclusions does she draw about God?

4. The author found self at the center of his hopelessness, his own dreams and expectations. Why does this focus lead to despair?

5. What does it mean to place our hope on God?

CHAPTER 5

MORPHING FEAR INTO COURAGE

A RE YOU CRYING again?" Mae's husband, Roberto, asked. "I'm scared," Mae confessed.

She could not hide the terror that filled her nights and days. There she was, in the middle of the night, her face in the pillow, trying to stifle sobs.

Mae and her husband came to the United States in 1977. A woman came to her door and asked, "Would you like to study the Bible?" Mae agreed. When the woman, a member of a cult, came, she said, "The end of the world is coming." Her statement terrified Mae.

She followed her husband's advice and told various priests about her fears. Their answers proved confusing: "There's no evidence the world is ending soon." "You don't need to read the Bible." "You can't believe the Bible."

> God and His truth are our foundation for courage.

Because Roberto thought the Bible had caused her turmoil, he hid it in the garage. But Mae sought answers. Often she locked herself in the bathroom to cry and pray, embarrassed for her children to see her tears.

How could Mae be so immobilized by fear? How can we, at times, be paralyzed by fear?

FEAR CAN PARALYZE

Often fear is a healthy and understandable apprehension of real danger. I remember traveling too fast on a slick winter road. Suddenly the car in front of me braked, and I knew I was going to hit him. Fear gripped me. I grasped the steering wheel tighter, and pumped the brakes firmly but without locking them. I avoided a collision. In this situation, fear actually worked in my favor.

But unhealthy fear can dominate our lives, and at times paralyze us. It can cloud our lives with persistent anxiety, or cause major medical problems. Fear has many synonyms: worry, dread, apprehension, distress.

> Unhealthy fear can dominate our lives, and at times paralyze us.

LIVING IN FEAR

My own battle with fear surfaced often. Fear of others and their opinions immobilized me. At one point I overheard a couple of church leaders around a corner, criticizing me with a mocking attitude. I reeled and my face flushed. In the coming hours a sledgehammer of grief and pain hammered me. I struggled to go on with life and ministry. I felt as if I was in a deep pit with no way out. It took me weeks to recover.

I feared strong people who forced me to conform to their will. I did not have the emotional strength to contend with them. To resist others I had to resist their anger, which scorched me. I worried about how to fulfill the command for unity in the church. At times I did what the angry ones wanted just to keep peace, and make some attempt at unity.

I feared the future and my own abilities. "I can't handle it. I can't go on." I have shared about my struggle in my first church. I felt I was being rejected by the people and church I loved. Thoughts of suicide arose because my emotional pain was so excruciating. Despite the thoughts, I determined never to pursue that course. Sundays were agony, as I struggled through my morning message, wounded by angry looks and antagonistic actions.

Why Do I Live Here?

As a believer and a church leader, how could I allow myself to wallow in anxiety? My fears were more real than the seeming wispy, intangible things spoken of in the Bible. I found it difficult to grasp what it said and to find any application in my world of killers and bullets.

What does this have to do with significance? It was fear that blocked me from becoming who God wanted me to be and what He wanted me to accomplish; it hammered at my sense of who I was. I did not feel strong and courageous, but small and powerless.

When do you experience fear? Perhaps you dread work because of the rejection of your colleagues. Perhaps your marriage is deteriorating and you're terrified of losing everything. You may be a student on overload, having trouble entering the classroom. You may be a senior citizen dreading the loss of your health.

Five Excuses Driven by Fear

In Exodus 3-4, the Lord revealed Himself to Moses in the burning bush, affirmed His love for His people, and called Moses to be His messenger of rescue. But Moses refused God's call, worded in four objections. Fear had immobilized this great man, and his fears reflect the anxieties we often face.

> Paralyzed by fear, Moses rejected God's call.

In His call the Lord said, ". . . Go. I am sending you to Pharaoh to bring my people the Israelites out of Egypt" (Exodus 3:10). Listen to Moses' five expressions of fear:

- "Who am I, that I should go to Pharaoh and bring the Israelites out of Egypt?" (Exodus 3:11b). This is the cry of his personal inadequacy. He feared failure in the huge task assigned. His own people would surely reject him as a toady of Pharaoh's house. The Egyptians might execute him for murder. Monstrous uncertainties loomed as a spectre.

> Courage is the mental or moral strength to venture, persevere, or withstand danger, fear, or difficulty.

- "What if they ask me 'What is His name?' What shall I answer?" (Exodus 3:13b). He feared his people would seriously question his source of authority. Though his question centered on God's name and identity, it thinly covered his own fear of rejection. He knew who the Lord was, but doubted others would accept his declaration or him.

- "What if they do not believe me or listen to me and say, 'The LORD did not appear to you'?" (Exodus 4:1). In this broader objection; he agonizes over the people's response. He dreads his message and authority being questioned with a flood of demeaning criticism. His anxiety dismisses the Lord's promise in 3:18 that the elders of Israel would listen.
- "O Lord, I have never been eloquent, neither in the past nor since you have spoken to your servant. I am slow of speech and tongue" (Exodus 4:10). Notice his rising frustration. Though he fears his ineptness in public speaking, before he fled Egypt he saw himself as his people's rescuer (Acts 7:25). Whatever his qualifications, they were enough for the Lord, who called him.
- "O Lord, please send someone else to do it" (Exodus 4:13). Up to now Moses seems to be reasoning with the Lord in intellectual honesty, getting his questions answered. At this point, paralyzed by fear, he rejects God's call. In his mind, danger, rejection, and failure loom so large he cannot see God's provision as more real.

Four Foundations for Courage

Having observed Moses' paralysis, let me suggest that one opposite of fear is courage. Courage is the mental or moral strength to venture, persevere, or withstand danger, fear, or difficulty. I am not suggesting a reckless, mindless courage like a child jumping off a roof with an umbrella. I am pointing to a courage that is a way of life based on truth. The Lord gave Moses

> God's identity is our answer to fear, and our reason for courage.

a concrete foundation for such courage, worded in four powerful statements:

- "I Am who I Am" (Exodus 3:14a). God's revealed identity was not only Moses' answer when questioned, but his greatest personal provision. The Hebrew word *Ehyeh* (I am) is the same root as Yahweh or Jehovah, the name for God that expresses his self-existence and faithfulness. Perhaps to Moses the Lord's identity seemed no practical resource at all. But it was everything; the Almighty was his Lord, supply, counselor, strengthener, and comforter.

  What about my fear? If we have come to Christ, we are not only individuals, but are identified with Him. As we live for Him, He lives through us in all His unlimited resources and character. This is the primary foundation stone for living with courage and risk. God's identity is our answer to fear, and our reason for courage.

- "I will be with you" (Exodus 3:12a). This represents one of the Lord's most powerful promises. It was also given to Isaac, Jacob, Joshua, Gideon, Solomon, Isaiah, and to believers in Matthew 28:20. You may ask, "What is that worth? A warm fuzzy religious feeling? Give me something tangible like a division of troops!" But as you study the results of the promise, you will discover that God turned the world upside down on behalf of those given the promise. It was going to be true for Moses, as he led millions to freedom.

  What about my fear? God, in His infinite power, glory, and character, lives within His children. We are not alone. His presence answers questions about our inadequacy, because He is adequate. In His presence He is companionship, comfort, and direction. If we will obey Him and trust Him, He will turn the world upside down for us.

- "I Am has sent me to you" (Exodus 3:14b). The decision for this mission and its success was the responsibility of God. He was the one sending. God was not looking for policy guidance on the feasibility of the mission, or a discussion of the weakness of Moses' resume. Moses was taking orders, not giving them. And God was not asking Moses to assume responsibility for the outcome. He needed to rest completely on God's call and provision, and leave the results to God.

  What about my fear? We are not the sender, we are the sent. God is not looking for policy guidance on the weakness of our resume. Our call in life, and our success, or lack of it, is the responsibility of God. Our rest on God, who has called each of us, is our reason for boldness in living, and our antidote to fear.

- "Now go; For I will help you speak and will teach you what to say (Exodus 4:12). Here were two assurances. First, the Lord would supernaturally assist Moses to speak. He does not command Moses to be eloquent, but just speak the message. Interestingly, when Moses finally went to Egypt he had no difficulty communicating verbally. What he saw as another ground for fear proved no impediment. In the second part of the promise he learned that God would give him the message.

  What about my fear? The Lord has crafted the mosaic of our abilities. He enables those He gifts. We must yield to that enabling by discovering, strengthening, and strenuously using our gifts. We do it for His glory, our growth, and the benefit of others around us. God's enabling is our reason for courage.

What Moses Missed

With all these assurances, why didn't Moses sprint to Egypt, buoyed by all the promises of God? I think he missed the next step—obedience. Because he refused God's call, the Lord's anger was stirred: "Then the LORD's anger burned against Moses" (Exodus 4:14a).

Let me suggest a prayer that might reflect Moses' needed step of obedience: "Lord, I praise You for Your assurances, but You know I am scared out of my mind by my own inadequacies, and the dangers in Egypt. Nonetheless, I am strapping on my sandals, and stepping out to fulfill Your call. Here we go!"

Moses needed to move forward in obedience despite his paralyzing fears, based on God's identity, call, presence, and promises.

> Obedience to God transforms fear into courage.

Campus Crusade founder Bill Bright has said, "Faith is like a muscle. The more you exercise it, the bigger it grows." Let me suggest that faith will not grow if we just sit in our chairs and refuse to obey. In the New Testament, the word for faith is *pistos*, and part of the impact of the word is faithfulness—carrying out what God asks us to do. Obedience to God transforms fear into courage.

Will we still experience the emotion of fear? Earlier I mentioned Lynn and some of her battles. Lynn says, "I have had to crash through fear all my life." Even though fear is present, moving forward to obey is the key to overcoming it.

Fear Transformed to Courage

I started the chapter with the story of Mae, who was paralyzed with fear. One day she placed a garage sale radio on the top of her refrigerator, and accidentally tuned to a Christian radio station. Mae says, "I started understanding the truths I longed for; the story that Christ died for me touched me deeply." During a morning radio program, she obeyed the truth and asked Christ to be her Savior.

In subsequent days her fear was replaced with peace and joy as she began to grow in her faith. Her new life of courageous living in Christ saw her find a church family where she could grow, though she knew no one initially. Her continued faith and example saw first her children, and then her husband come to faith.

The answer for immobilizing fear is, "I Am that I Am." He calls us, promises His presence, and enables us for every challenge. He is our foundation for courage. In His power, we obey.

Think It Through

1. Why would a believer have to face fear when intellectually he knows he has all the resources of God?

2. Facing the daily agonies of life, do the promises of Scripture ever seem intangible and unreal? What promises are most difficult for you to implement?

3. Summarize Moses' fears. What is a consistent focus throughout his questions and objections?

4. How are the Lord's answers the great provision for our own battle with fear?

5. How can fear be turned to courage? How is it possible when all the obstacles and difficulties in life remain?

CHAPTER 6

BIRTHING HEALING OUT OF GRIEF

O UR PARENTS THOUGHT if they waited until we kids went to bed, we would not hear. We heard every word, cringing in our beds, almost vibrating to every shouted word. Mom and Dad were fighting again. Often the arguments centered on how they were going to pay the bills. But the significance to us was greater than finances. *What will we do when our home breaks up tomorrow?* I agonized. *Where will I go? Where will my brother and sisters go? Will they keep us together or split us up?* Though my parents never did separate, uncertainty filled my world. Security hung by a fragile thread. The conflict spawned grief that lasted well into adulthood.

But isn't grief associated with the death of a loved one? Physical death is not the only source of this powerful response to adversity. Grief is a normal, God-given reaction to loss, death, or change. It may be a financial loss, deterioration in health, or a

> . . . A good definition of grief is anxiety provoked by loss.

loss of self-esteem. But normally the loss centers on the significant change of a relationship. A good definition of grief is anxiety provoked by loss.

After the end of World War II, researchers studied young children separated from their mothers, usually during a temporary hospitalization. Initially the boys and girls protested by crying and calling out for their mothers. Some ran after them or searched for them. The next phase was extreme distress, sobbing inconsolably, followed by withdrawal into self and unwillingness to interact with others. These separation behaviors are expressions of grief. My own grief was an emotional anticipation of separation.

> Normally the loss centers on the significant change of a relationship.

GRIEF: A COMMON HUMAN EXPERIENCE

For most of my life I was not aware that grief remained from my childhood. Five years ago, at a crisis point, I picked up *The Grief Recovery Handbook*, at that time authored by Friedmann and Cherry. As I read I discovered the memories of my parents' conflicts as well as layers of grief from many phases of life. I remembered the threats of a childhood teacher, my dad's disappointed expectations of my being a sports star, and the split in my first church. These incidents formed a heavy burden that had accumulated, layer upon layer, until I felt I could not go on with life or ministry. My grief was not unique: grief is a painful and common human experience.

- *Recognize the Symptoms of Grief.* Are you bearing the symptoms of grief? My grief was evidenced by an underlying sadness. For others, loss may cause intense emotional suffering, accompanied by a sense of shock and paralysis that can incapacitate one for the normal functions of life. Some may weep, become depressed, or condemn themselves. It is also common to become angry with God, others, or oneself.

Grief produced a loss of hope that made it difficult to go on.

Grief also produced a loss of hope within me that made it difficult for me to go on. The future appeared to be a long dark tunnel without end, never seeing the light and beauty of day. The load I carried hampered my search for my identity and giftedness.

- *Explore the Source of Your Grief.* Go back to the incidents that caused your pain. I realize this may be difficult. Someone may respond, "I cannot face it; it is too painful." Remember that we are people of truth. Jesus said His person and ministry were characterized by truth (John 14:6, 17; 16:13). God's truth is where we find our healing. I found as I faced these incidents, instead of burying them, God was already ministering to me.

   I tried to remember each incident that produced a sense of loss. As it came to the surface I began to see it in the light of God's truth. In some incidents unkind, insensitive, or proud people had inflicted pain. In other cases, I brought pain on myself by my own actions. Tragic circumstances and flawed relationships can heighten our pain.

- *Acknowledge the Depth of Your Feelings.* I had not only stuffed my feelings of emotional pain, I had failed to recognize the depth of feelings from each incident. Many direct us to deny or minimize the depth of our anguish: "It's really not as bad as all that." "Get over it!" When a child's pet dies, a well-meaning parent may try to replace the loss, but fail to validate the child's perception of their loss: "Don't feel bad. We can get another pet." Worse, they may criticize the child's grief: "Get over it, it is only a dog!" But my pain could not be resolved with glib advice or my attempts to put it behind me. I needed to acknowledge it.

GOD, THE INFINITE GRIEVER

We must realize that God is the great griever. While I was denying my feelings and trying to get past them, God was a friend who longed to come alongside and validate the reality and depth of my feelings. The fact that God shared this emotion with me became part of my healing. When Israel turned from God to serve idols, Jeremiah wept with the Lord over His lost child:

God is the great griever.

> Oh, that my head were a spring of water and my eyes a fountain of tears! I would weep day and night . . .
>
> —Jeremiah 9:1a

Jeremiah's book, Lamentations, is a complete expression of the Lord's sorrow and his own. Isn't God above such painful feelings? The Bible shows that God is a person with mind, emotions, and will (although infinite, in each case). Emotions are a part of His nature. And this emotional side is true of all three persons of the Trinity. For example, it is possible to grieve the Holy Spirit (Ephesians 4:30).

CHRIST'S OWN GRIEF

A very unique side of God's grieving is that of the Son of Man.

> He was despised and forsaken of men, A man of sorrows and acquainted with grief.
>
> —Isaiah 53:3a (NASB)

This Messianic passage talks about Christ's personal grief. If the emotion stems from lost or changed relationships, what could be its source for the Savior? Consider the cross and the events of Christ's Passion:

> After he had said this, Jesus was troubled in spirit and testified, "I tell you the truth, one of you is going to betray me."
>
> —John 13:21

Christ loved Judas, as He does all human beings, and longed for him to repent. Judas' betrayal wounded the Savior.

I also find Him sorrowing in the rejection of His nation: "As he approached Jerusalem and saw the city, he wept over it" (Luke 19:41).

Though the Triumphal Entry was Christ's presenting Himself as king, as He entered the city, He wept. The reason? "He came to that which was his own, but his own did not receive him" (John 1:11).

But His deepest sorrow is seen on the cross:

> From the sixth hour until the ninth hour darkness came over all the land. About the ninth hour Jesus cried out in a loud voice, "Eloi, Eloi, lama sabachthani?"—which means, "My God, my God, why have you forsaken me?"
>
> —Matthew 27:45-46

Fellowship between the Father and the Son was broken because the Son carried our sin. This break also accounts for Christ's agony in the garden. Because the bond with His father was infinite, His grief was without measure.

CHRIST CARRIED OUR GRIEF

Christ not only bears His own personal burden of grief, but He carries the sorrows of others: "Surely our griefs He Himself bore, and our sorrows He carried" (Isaiah 53:4a NASB). This refers not only to His payment for sin on the cross, but that as a friend He can bear deeply the pain of a friend; He is touched deeply by our sufferings. The word for grief is the Hebrew word that comes from the root, *chalah* that has a base meaning of sickness, but applies to a host of other weaknesses, griefs, and sorrows.

> Christ not only carries His own grief, but ours as well.

Was the audience correct in saying it was because of His love for Lazarus that Jesus wept at the tomb of Lazarus (John 11:35)? If His mourning was due to Lazarus' physical death, did He not realize he would raise Lazarus back to life? The passage itself gives us a most important clue. It says the grief of Mary and the others who had come with her moved Him to share their grief (John 11:33).

Hebrews also shows Christ, as a high priest, bearing our weakness:

For we do not have a high priest who is unable to sympathize with our weaknesses . . .

—Hebrews 4:15a

THE RESOLUTION OF GRIEF

- *Share Your Grief with a Friend.* Talking about your loss is a beginning step toward recovery. In communicating to another, it assists the griever in discovering his pain and loss. I tended to hole up and try to heal myself. Though that method produced rich fellowship with the Lord, isolation from fellow sufferers proved unhelpful. As I included others in my discoveries, we shared together, and mutual healing began. A friend with whom I shared, had also battled grief, and began to teach a course on grief recovery. I taught the topic to caregivers, published an article, and shared the journey of healing with my congregation. The communication became part of my own healing.

> Sharing with another assists in discovering and healing the pain of loss.

- *Share Your Grief with God.* Tell God of your pain, just as you have shared with your friend. Recognize that He not only knows your anguish, but suffers with you. David records: "You have taken account of my wanderings; Put my tears in Your bottle. Are they not in Your book?" (Psalm 56:8 NASB).

  I have found great benefit in recording these prayers in a journal. The Scriptures exhort us to tell God everything and also to cast all our cares upon Him. This means that we now give to Him our emotional load *and* the responsibility for acting to heal or resolve the problem.

- *Forgive Others.* When my church split and some sought the end of my ministry, it hurt deeply. But though I was

> I found freedom in releasing my animosity toward those who had wounded me.

quick to point out the failings of others, I was not without blame. Over a period of months, I found freedom in releasing my animosity toward those who had wounded me. Someone has said, "The person who is bitter is always wrong." Forgiveness is not a declaration of their innocence. It does not mean you are blind to character, failures, or frailties of others. But you release your case against them to the One who alone is the Judge.

- *Minister Healing to Others.* When I exhort people in pain to minister to others, the reaction is often, "When I am healed and whole, then I can help others. How can I give what I do not have?" God's healing is most fully experienced when we, the wounded, step out to heal others. The wounded healer is also the most effective minister; in giving, the love and obedience expended accelerates one's own restoration to health. As you comfort others with the comfort you have received, you will experience a growing sense of joy and fulfillment (2 Corinthians 1:3-4).

ONE END OF THE JOURNEY

As I dealt truthfully with the sources of my grief, such as conflict in my home, I began one of the most powerful healing journeys in my life. The Lord encouraged me to examine the pain I had hidden. I sensed God saying, "Yes, you really were devastated by those things. I grieve with you." Where sadness had plagued me, a new joy and release began to occur. The Man of Sorrows had become acquainted with my grief, taken it upon Himself, and in its place gave me wholeness. And the result went beyond me. I found joy in helping others by bearing their grief with them (Galatians 6:2). Then I saw the opportunity to bear some of the burden that God himself carries. Remembering how He invited His disciples to join Him in His grief in the Garden of Gethsemane, I found myself yielding to bear some of His sorrows.

As long as we live, painful events, loss, and change will intersect our lives. Just as our Lord bore a constant load of grief, so will we, but we can grieve resting on Him:

> Brothers, we do not want you to be ignorant about those who fall asleep, or to grieve like the rest of men, who have no hope.
> —1 Thessalonians 4:13

This separates us from all others who grieve. We grieve in hope. Despite sorrows, we can live in constant health and healing as God ministers to our spirits, walks with us, and causes us to joy in His future for us. Our healing can be part of God's miracle in the lives of others as we come alongside to help, and even share the burden of grief our God carries, who bore and bears all for us.

We grieve in hope.

Think It Through

1. In addition to the death of a loved one, what other sort of deaths cause grief?

2. What have been the most significant sources of grief for you?

3. Does it seem strange to you that God grieves? What are some of the sources of God's grief?

4. How can others help heal the pain of loss? Why do we sometimes isolate ourselves in pain, instead of seeking the healing of fellowship?

5. Why is it important for the wounded to extend healing to others?

CHAPTER 7

DISCERNING THE VOICE OF OUR ENEMY

AS A MILITARY pilot, I had a successful career and had chosen what could be a lifelong profession. But in 1971 and 1972, my wife, Beverly, and I felt the Lord directing us to Bible training to prepare for a life of ministry. I submitted my resignation to the Air Force and enrolled in seminary.

We rented a small apartment near the Dallas, Texas, seminary that was adequate for our small family, now including our nine-month-old son, David. But as I began my final paperwork for entrance, a cloud of doubt gripped me, oppressing me like a powerful storm. Voices I had fought all my life whispered, *What are you doing here? Who do you think you are fooling? You aren't some model, victorious Christian. What a farce. You are a fine example of a holy life. Are you forgetting how often you fail? Now you will fail at this. What makes you think you are smart enough to make it through a graduate program with a language emphasis?*

Whose voice is it?

Many times I fell to my knees in our little apartment, crying out to God. Was it His voice sending me in a different direction? Had I misunderstood what the Lord wanted for us? Or was it the voice of the enemy slandering me and trying to block God's call? I asked myself, *Whose voice is it?*

One of the most puzzling experiences of life is discerning the voice of God—who unconditionally loves us—from the slanders and accusations of Satan. At times we all battle voices and doubts. They come from many sources, not just from the enemy, but from our own conscience, family, and peers. If we are to be the people we are called to be, it is crucial we discern the voice of our spiritual enemy, and discern its difference from the encouraging voice of our God who calls us.

SATAN THE ACCUSER

We should not be surprised that the enemy attacks us. Satan's name means *adversary*. He is called the accuser of the saints (Revelation 12:10), who continually accuses us before God, and to our face, within our conscience. He attacks not only to defeat us but to dishonor the God we serve.

What kind of situations in our lives might be occasions of his attack? The book of Job is instructive about one platform.

Attack Opportunity #1—Adversity

Satan brought extreme adversity to Job to attempt to get him to curse and dishonor God. To get a bigger picture of his objective, consider Satan's accusations of Job in the courtroom of heaven. Job's character, faith, and prominent position as a visible servant of God made him a natural target.

"Does Job fear God for nothing?" Satan replied. "Have you not put a hedge around him and his household and everything he has? You have blessed the work of his hands, so that his flocks and herds are spread throughout the land. But stretch out your hand and strike everything he has, and he will surely curse you to your face."

—Job 1:9-11

Allowed by God, Job entered his furnace of affliction, but did not know that Satan was the one imposing it. The attack included the death of his children, the loss of his wealth, and the loss of health, including severe boils. Then his mental anguish was heightened by the despair of his wife and the slander of friends. In the contest between Satan and God, let me summarize the accusations of the enemy, and the affirmation of the Lord:

> Satan uses great trials to lure us to doubt God and dishonor Him.

Enemy's Voice: Though you are innocent (29:14, 17), God has afflicted you and abandoned you (29:2-6). Curse God and die (2:9).

God's Voice: You are my choice servant (1:8; 42:8-9). Walk with me in adversity, even as you have in blessing.

Perhaps these voices sound familiar to you. When faced with adversity and suffering, I spent years wallowing in self pity, wrongly proclaiming my own innocence, and implying that God had abandoned me and afflicted me unfairly. Yet when I returned to the Lord's affirmations, I was surrounded by His love, encouragement, and assurance of my place and call.

Satan is our adversary and uses calamity to discourage us from God's path, and lure us to dishonor Him. Let's look at another picture of his opposition.

Attack Opportunity #2—Our Unworthiness

Satan's attack on Joshua the high priest reveals another base of our enemy's attack—our own sinfulness and unworthiness.

> Then he showed me Joshua the high priest standing before the angel of the LORD, and Satan standing at his right hand to accuse him. The LORD said to Satan, "The LORD rebuke you, Satan! Indeed, the LORD who has chosen Jerusalem rebuke you! Is this not a brand plucked from the fire?" Now Joshua was clothed with filthy garments and standing before the angel. He spoke and said to those who were standing before him, saying, "Remove the filthy garments from him."
>
> —Zechariah 3:1-4a NASB

The basis of Satan's attack on Joshua was the unclean clothing he wore. It was a travesty of the high priest's depiction of holiness and purity. The assault had greater significance than just the person of Joshua. The Jewish nation had been restored to their land, but restoring the priesthood after captivity presented countless problems from a tarnished chapter in Jewish history. The Lord's gracious declaration of cleansing intervened to solve the problem.

Satan will use our unworthiness to slander and discourage us.

Let me again summarize the nature of the attack, and the contrasting voice of God:

Enemy's Voice: Who are you to presume to be high priest? You are sinful, unclean, unworthy (Zechariah 3:4).

God's Voice: I have cleansed you and called you. Walk with me and perform my service (Zechariah 3:7).

Satan, himself the leader of the heavenly rebellion against God, accuses each of us of our sinfulness and unworthiness. He will use our undeservedness to slander and discourage us: "Have you noticed what a rotten sinner you are? There, you failed again!"

Are we unworthy sinners? Of course. We have all sinned and missed God's standard, but those who have believed on Christ are completely cleansed at the cross of Christ—the total payment for sin (Appendix 1). When we sin as children of God, the Lord would have us confess our sin as soon as we are aware of it, receive His cleansing, and live in victory empowered by God.

Assault Opportunity #3—Our Call and Honor

At the very beginning of our Lord's ministry, during Jesus' temptation in the wilderness (Matthew 4:1-11), Satan confronted Jesus privately and personally. Did Satan appear to Him or just speak to Him inwardly? We do not know. But the attack was real. Hebrews records that the Lord was tempted in every way that we are (Hebrews 4:15). He did not yield to *any* temptation, but was genuinely tempted.

Enemy's Voice: You are not the Son of God (Matthew 4:3, 6), but a lowly human worm. The Father has robbed you of the glory you deserve (4:5-6). Worship me and the world will worship you (4:9).

Father's Voice: You are My Beloved Son, Infinite God, Messiah. I am well pleased with You (3:17).

Just as Satan failed to acknowledge Christ's deity (He is God), and his Messianic call as the King of Israel, so he uses our identity and call as an attack point. To the Savior he implies that the Father has denied the Son glory or blessing, and offers a quick, though disobedient way to gain glory and recognition.

> One of Satan's potent strategies is to attack our call by denying it or mutilating it.

One of Satan's potent strategies is to attack our call by denying it or mutilating it. Just as he sought to diminish the Son of God with his slander, so he tries to reduce our stature as children of God. Often this intimidates us, and our pride springs to defend us. Instead, we must trust the God who loves us and cling with bulldog tenacity to who we are in Him.

Attack Opportunity #4—Failure

In chapter one, we saw the great discouragement of Elijah the prophet, as seen in 1 Kings 19. We saw his crushing despair at the death of his dream. Now let's view it as an attack of the enemy, Satan.

Enemy's Voice: You have failed and will never bring revival (19:4). Give up and die (19:4). Despite your zeal, God has not supported you. Unless you flee, Jezebel (the ungodly queen) will kill you (19:10, 14).

God's Voice: I have called you and have significant work for you to do (1 Kings 17:1-4, 9; 18:1; 19:15-18).

When Jezebel's threat revealed there had not been the whole-hearted turning to God Elijah had dreamed of, he yielded to Satan's temptation to give up. Elijah's despondency also shows that he was at the center of his dreams of revival.

How often am I at the center of my dreams? I may profess that my concern is for God's glory and His cause, yet often I find a persistent rebellious longing to be successful—that I be enthroned. We may long for some ideal state with ourselves at the center, just as Adam and Eve were lured by the promise that they could become as God.

> Many times *we* are at the center of our dreams, a flaw the enemy may expose and build upon.

Through Elijah's words and actions, I see him accusing God of not showing up for him. Many times my attitude reflects the same: "I did the best I could, but God did not come through for me!" This may not be blasphemy, but it's certainly dishonoring to God.

Whose Voice Is It?

Here are some clues to distinguish the voice of the Lord from the voice of the enemy:

- *God's voice brings peace.* He is a friend coming alongside, a loving parent (Hebrews 2:14-15). Satan's accusations bring fear, turmoil, doubt, and confusion instead of peace.
- *God's voice encourages.* He seeks to restore, equip, and spur you on to fruitfulness and victory. The enemy seeks to discourage, defeat, and set you aside from usefulness. "What's the use! Why not give up?"
- *God's voice is always specific.* Satan's accusation may start with the specific but points to the general and the negative.

"You always fail!" "You are weak now, and you will always be weak. Give up!"

- *God's voice is one of hope and trust in God.* Satan's voice is one of unbelief and doubt, not only in God, but also in His work within you. "This is a disaster. You are put to shame again. God has failed you."

- *The Spirit points to and glorifies God.* Satan's goal is to discredit God (Genesis 3:1-5). He aims for your defeat because it will dishonor God.

- *God's voice, even in correction, affirms we are loved as His children (Hebrews 12:5-11).* The enemy judges and condemns us, and slanders our place and our call, just as he accused Joshua the high priest.

- *God's voice speaks forgiveness and restoration* (1 John 1:9) while the enemy speaks condemnation (Romans 8:33-34).

- *God's voice strengthens us* to live in confidence in Him and do His work (Luke 22:31-32). The enemy seeks to weaken us.

RESISTING THE VOICE OF THE ENEMY

How should we respond when confronted with the voice of the enemy? Consider the exhortation of James:

> Submit yourselves, then, to God. Resist the devil, and he will flee from you. Come near to God and he will come near to you. Wash your hands, you sinners, and purify your hearts, you double-minded.
>
> —James 4:7-8

I find in the Lord Jesus the best example of resisting Satan's attack. He firmly set his purpose to serve the Father alone (Hebrews 10:5-7). In fasting and prayer, he nurtured his fellowship with the Father, and nourished Himself on Scripture. He discerned the voice of the enemy and resisted it. He refused the temptation to seek His own glory, but honored His Father in everything. Finally, He commanded Satan to flee (Matthew 4:10).

GOD, OUR SOURCE OF VICTORY

Though the attack of the enemy at seminary was the most powerful I had ever experienced, God enabled me to identify it, and to persist in His calling. Though the attack lasted for two to three weeks, I cast myself on God and His Word. Listening for, and resisting the voice of the enemy, is a lifelong process for all of us. Often we are fooled, or choose to yield to Satan's slander, discouragement, or blasphemy of our call.

Often I have misidentified the nature of the victory I should seek. I longed for a victory on the mountain top with my fist in the air—a complete conquest—a cessation of conflict. I have discovered that real victory is remaining in the battle, fighting, yes, sometimes losing, but marching on with the armor and resources God has given to us until we experience the ultimate victory:

> Then I heard a loud voice in heaven say: "Now have come the salvation and the power and the kingdom of our God, and the authority of his Christ. For the accuser of our brothers, who accuses them before our God day and night, has been hurled down. They overcame him by the blood of the Lamb and by the word of their testimony; they did not love their lives so much as to shrink from death."
>
> —Revelation 12:10-11

Think It Through

1. When in life have the competing inward voices confused you?

2. Why does Satan attack when we are battling against great adversity?

3. How can Satan use our feelings of unworthiness? Are we unworthy?

4. How can failure be an opportune platform for Satan's attack?

5. What clues help you distinguish the voice of the enemy from the voice of God?

THE FLESH THAT HINDERS US

CHAPTER 8

UNLEASHING POWER IN FRAILTY

IRCUMSTANCES CLOSED IN and trapped Connie, a young mother. Her family of five, including three small children, lived in an apartment in a poor part of town. She taught second grade, riding a bike to school, as they had no car. Her husband, unemployed, had recently been injured at the steel plant. Then she became pregnant. How could she take time off when she was the only source of income? Powerless to change her situation, she wrote, "Things are absolutely the worst! No car. Riding bike to school each day. Now I'm pregnant." She went to her pastor's wife and sobbed. The wise counselor said, "God has put a difficult mountain in front of you. But if you endure, there will be a blessing at the end."

> Things are absolutely the worst!

Do you feel powerless and immobilized? Perhaps you are like Lynn who said, "I remember feeling lonely . . . even in a crowded room. It felt like nobody wanted to know me, or that I was worthy to know." Lisa felt powerless in middle age: "At forty-one, I had run out of all my expected roles. I questioned my significance . . . feeling invisible." Jeanne felt powerless in losing her husband to cancer, and her daughter to mental illness. Many of us feel handicapped by low emotional or physical resources. For some, it may stem from trauma in childhood or blows suffered in other phases of life. The sense of powerlessness devastates our sense of significance.

> I remember feeling lonely . . . even in a crowded room. It felt like nobody wanted to know me, or that I was worthy to know.

Thinking and communicating about our weaknesses is uncomfortable. Why would we talk about our frailties when we can boast of our strengths? It may seem an unwieldy topic, vague, and difficult to define. No matter how self-sufficient we may feel, we all know our weaknesses are forces powerful enough to paralyze us.

POWERLESSNESS ILLUSTRATED IN SCRIPTURE

- *Jewish warriors felt immobilized* facing Goliath and the Philistine forces in battle.

On hearing the Philistine's words, Saul and all the Israelites were dismayed and terrified.
—1 Samuel 17:11

Sadly, this paralysis had nothing to do with their lack of physical ability or God's inability to strengthen them, but to fear partially induced by Goliath's intimidating threat.

- *Paul confessed great weakness.* Though originally a powerful Jewish leader, after encountering persecution and opposition, Paul admits:

When I came to you, brothers, I did not come with eloquence or superior wisdom as I proclaimed to you the testimony about God . . . I came to you in weakness and fear, and with much trembling.

—1 Corinthians 2:1-3

- *Though Jesus Christ is God, in His earthly form He demonstrated weakness.* It was His weakness in the fasting (for forty days) and temptation . . . . But His greatest moment of weakness seemed to come in the Garden of Gethsemane, facing the trial of the cross. The reality of His weakened condition is highlighted by the angel who came to strengthen Him (Luke 22:43).

Now let's consider the frailties that beset all of us.

How Are We Weak?

As humans, we are weak in countless ways. Our minds can be powerful tools for good, and were created to know God. But our mental capabilities have many limitations. Often we do not perceive things correctly. We may believe our perceptions, but often we are sincerely wrong. Our conclusions are an always changing, fragile veil influenced by experience, training, and the blows we have suffered. In Genesis 3:1-5, Eve believed in the lie of Satan and ate the fruit.

Our emotions can powerfully move us to feel what others feel or what God feels, and move us to action. But our emotions can also be weak. Often they seem like a roller coaster running out of control to heights and depths. They can lead us away from truth and sensitize us to things that should not trouble us, and deaden us to emotions we should sense deeply.

Though our wills are powerful forces that can move nations and accomplish great good, the human will is often in rebellion against God. All of us are weak when facing temptation. Speaking of the struggle of all believers, Paul says: ". . . the sinful nature desires what is contrary to the Spirit, and the Spirit what is contrary to the sinful nature. They are in conflict with each other, so that you do not do what you want" (Galatians 5:17). In addition, Satan, our powerful enemy, exploits our weaknesses.

Our faith is also weak at times, just like the father who was challenged by Jesus about his faith, when his son desperately needed healing. The father admitted, "I do believe; help me overcome my unbelief!" (Mark 9:24).

What is the greatest of our frailties? Perhaps assuming we have none. Oswald Chambers says, "A self-assured saint is of no value to God. He is abnormal, unfit for daily life, and completely unlike God" (My Utmost for His Highest, May 1).

> Though we are created perfect according to God's design, our frailties are a part of God's plan.

We may feel powerless when we face great obstacles or challenges we cannot solve with our own resources. We measure ourselves, and come up short. When confronted with great challenges, Paul said, "We despaired even of life . . ." (see 2 Corinthians 1:8-11).

The weakness I am speaking of is not physical weakness, but that of mind, emotions, will, or spirit. It can be a lack of ability or perceived lack of it, producing a deficit in our confidence. The word for strength in Hebrew is *hayil*, and means the ability to affect or produce. Weakness is the absence of that ability.

CREATED WITH WEAKNESS?

Though we are created perfect according to God's design, our frailties are a part of God's plan. This is not just true of those created with obvious handicaps, but all of us. Though Psalm 139:13-16 describes us as "fearfully and wonderfully made" and "skillfully wrought," 1 Corinthians 15:42-44 also describes the human body as perishable and characterized by weakness.

> Our weaknesses are not some cosmic mistake.

Jesus and His disciples encountered a man with obvious frailty, a man blind from birth. The disciples mistakenly assumed that his blindness was due to sin. They asked, "Rabbi, who sinned, this man for his parents, that he was born blind?"

"Neither this man nor his parents sinned," said Jesus, "but this happened so that the work of God might be displayed in his life" (John 9:1-3).

Just as with this man, our weaknesses are not some cosmic mistake. Even our frailties are designed by Him for our good, a blessing for others around us, and for His own glory. Though God knows the reason for each frailty, our understanding is imperfect, and we dare not give quick, stereotyped answers pronouncing God's purpose for each.

Not only have we inherited a damaged package, but our own wrong choices and personal sin further contribute to our flaws. This is most obvious in choices such as drug addiction, alcoholism, immorality, and crime, which damage others and the individual. The sins and wrongs of others that impact us weaken us even more. An example is abuse in the home, where children bear their scars for life.

WEAKNESS TURNED TO STRENGTH

Scripture declares that God can turn abject human weakness into strength, so we can live in a confidence we could never possess on our own.

> And what more shall I say? I do not have time to tell about Gideon, Barak, Samson, Jepthah, David, Samuel and the prophets, who through faith conquered kingdoms, administered justice, and gained what was promised; who shut the mouths of lions, quenched the fury of the flames, and escaped the edge of the sword; whose weakness was turned to strength . . .
> —Hebrews 11:32-34a

Strengthening must necessarily start with seeing our lack.

Why were these people able to accomplish such notable feats, considering the passage indicates their natural weakness? Due to their obedience to God, He supernaturally strengthened each one. And what God did for these Old Testament saints, He desires to do for anyone who will believe Him and serve Him.

But this supernatural strengthening must begin with the willingness to see and acknowledge our lack—our many limitations and inabilities. Though we do not have a full assessment of our deficits (only God does), the truth about our weaknesses is the starting place for strength.

Isaiah talks about the Lord strengthening those who place their trust in God:

> But those who hope in the LORD will renew their strength. They will soar on wings like eagles; they will run and not grow weary, they will walk and not be faint.
> —Isaiah 40:31

ALLOW GOD TO STRENGTHEN YOU

If we know God and align ourselves with Him and His plan, He infuses His strength into us. God gives to us something beyond our own resources. As Paul said, "I can do everything through him who gives me strength" (Philippians 4:13).

The measure of the power available to us is the measure of the infinite ability it took to raise Christ from the dead:

> The measure of the power available to us is the measure of the infinite ability it took to raise Christ from the dead.

> That power is like the working of his mighty strength, which he exerted in Christ when he raised him from the dead and seated him at his right hand in the heavenly realms . . .
> —Ephesians 1:19b-20

You may say, "I know the Lord, and yet still feel weak!" Here is what I know to be true, from Scripture and my own experience. Strength is simply God giving us the ability to do His will. That's it! It's not bulging biceps, towering home runs, or charisma that captures the hearts of thousands, but the ability to do God's will.

STRENGTHEN YOURSELF WITH GOD'S HELP

- *Strengthen your mind.* We strengthen our mental faculties when we turn away from confused human reasoning, and focus our minds on God and His truth. We can choose where we place our mental focus.

> Since, then, you have been raised with Christ, set your hearts on things above, where Christ is seated at the right hand of God. Set your minds on things above, not on earthly things.
> —Colossians 3:1-2

A starting place is reading, studying, and memorizing portions of Scripture, especially those that pertain to your situation. Group Bible studies are a great encouragement in this process, either at church or in home groups. As we turn away from the world's thinking and place our mind on God's truths, our minds are transformed (Romans 12:1-2).

- *Strengthen your emotions.* Part of God's provision for our emotional healing is to take our entire range of emotions to God, place ourselves in a position of dependence on Him, then grow in feeling what God feels. The Lament Psalms exemplify an anguished soul pouring out his distress to God. God, an emotional being Himself, understands the cry of the human heart, and offers Himself as a perfect provision.

> Come to Me all you who are weary and burdened, and I will give you rest.
> —Matthew 11:28

A great resource for our emotions is to consider how greatly we are loved by God.

- *Strengthen your will.* Our wills often seem capricious, selfish, and ungovernable. The carefully observed example of others has a powerful effect on our own purpose. The impact goes far beyond lessons taught in a classroom.

  Paul's example powerfully affected Timothy, and he in turn was instructed to mentor others (2 Timothy 2:1-3). Believers are exhorted to steel their wills by following the supreme example of Christ:

Let us fix our eyes on Jesus, the author and perfecter of our faith, who for the joy set before him endured the cross, scorning its shame, and sat down at the right hand of the throne of God. Consider him who endured such opposition from sinful men, so that you will not grow weary and lose heart.

—Hebrews 12:2-3

ALLOW OTHERS TO HELP STRENGTHEN YOU

One of the most powerful forces of encouragement and strengthening is the friendship and fellowship of others. Have you had times when the prayer, support, or gifts of others encouraged you in a profound way? In his classic book *Building Up One Another*, Gene Getz shares his discovery of the "one anothers" of the New Testament. They are the commands to believers to love and build up one another. This mutual selfless giving can form a powerful foundation of support, enabling us to discover our value and giftedness.

But you may say, "Many believers I know are not loving. I have been hurt by many of them." You only have control over what you can do. You can build the framework of love in your own life, then demonstrate it to others. The Bible says, "A man that hath friends must show himself friendly . . ." (Proverbs 18:24a KJV).

The chapter opened with the story of Connie, desperately frail in her hour of need. Her pregnancy produced a fourth child,

Bill, who proved a great comfort to her following the early death of her husband. Connie modeled Christlike character, taught the Scriptures, and after retirement gave herself tirelessly to ministry. From her weakness, God birthed true strength and victory. He can do the same for you.

Think It Through

1. When have you felt powerless and immobilized?

2. How are we weak in our mind, emotions, and will? How does sin further weaken us in those resources?

3. Why did God create us with areas of inability?

4. In Heb. 11:32-34, in what sense was the weakness of these heroes turned to strength? How could it be strength if some were tortured or were martyred?

5. Though aware of your own weakness, why invest time and effort to strengthen others?

CHAPTER 9

OVERCOMING A GREAT WEAKNESS

D ENNIS HELPED FOUND pioneer firms in the computer industry. Having graduated from college in 1972, in San Francisco, he started his career in Silicon Valley. In a rocket ride of eleven years his company went from zero to $3 billion in sales. The fever to build computers and sell them was even called Silicon Valley Fever.

But Dennis battled another sickness, alcoholism. The struggle began in college, and now, in a surging industry, each sales call meant cocktails, and reaching a sales goal initiated a kegger. Alcohol and stress led him to cocaine, and his world collapsed. Having lost a fortune of $3-4 million, he ended up under a bridge in Aptos, California. At one point, covered with his own vomit, others under the bridge mocked, "Look at him. He says he was a computer CEO!"

> Exasperating are the personal weaknesses that cling to us and hobble us.

Exasperating are the personal weaknesses that cling to us and hobble us. We all have them, and periodically they take us to the mat. We feel we cannot possibly go on. They humble us before God, others, and ourselves.

SOME NEVER WIN

Some people never win the battle. Early in his life Richard had joined friends in "huffing"—spraying inhalants into a bag, and breathing the fumes to produce a high. It was well known that the practice damaged the heart. Now in his mid twenties, because of his continued substance abuse, his wife and three boys went to live with family. Richard, discouraged, again turned to inhalants, and died of heart failure at age twenty-six.

WE ALL BATTLE THORNS

Periodically, I trim branches off rose bushes in my yard. I often seek to trim a cane or branch from the inside of a bush. Convinced that I can reach through a narrow opening in the bush, I am usually pricked by one or more thorns. Recently I carried one thorn or splinter with me for a period of days; it was so small that I could not easily remove it, but I always knew it was there.

Our battle often devastates our sense of significance, and repeatedly humbles us.

We are always aware of our greatest personal weakness. What is yours? Over a long period of time mine was depression—the unbelieving, fear-based thought life that issued from wrong conclusions about myself. You may daily battle with anger, fear, substances, or lack of discipline. Internet pornography may devastate your thought life. As you win some battles and lose others, your area of greatest weakness may change.

Paul described the intensity of his own battle:

> I do not understand what I do. For what I want to do I do not do, but what I hate I do. . . For I have the desire to do what is good, but I cannot carry it out. For what I do is not the good I want to do; no, the evil I do not want to do—this I keep on doing. . . What a wretched man I am! Who will rescue me from this body of death?
>
> —Romans 7:15-24

His exclamation about the body of death may refer to the practice of Romans to tie a prisoner to a dead body, face to face, body to body, limbs to limbs. In a relatively short period of time the live prisoner was dead also; death had overcome life. Our battle often feels like being tied to death, our weakness devastates our sense of significance, and repeatedly humbles us.

FEELINGS OF DEFEAT

As a young believer, when I battled areas of temptation, I would often hear the enemy's mocking whisper, *There! You did it again! Can't you see how weak you are? You will never have victory.* I felt a continual sense of defeat. To a friend of mine, struggling with areas of obedience, the voice of the enemy says, *How can you be a believer if you fail like that?*

In their discouragement, throughout the centuries some people have decided that since our mind and body fails us, it should be made to suffer. I lived for three years in the Philippines. At some religious parades people could be seen flagellating themselves with whips, and allowing themselves to be mounted on crosses with nails driven through their hands. Their self-inflicted suffering was an ill-conceived attempt to atone for their sins, so great was their sense of need.

GOD RELEASES THE OPPRESSED

God has provided for those who cry for release from their struggle with sin. God's very nature relates to delivering those who struggle. Early in Christ's earthly ministry, He went to Nazareth where He had been raised. He was handed the scroll of Isaiah out of which He read Isaiah 61:1-2 (recorded in Luke 4:16-21):

> The Spirit of the Lord is on me, because he has anointed me to preach good news to the poor. He has sent me to proclaim freedom for the prisoners and recovery of sight for the blind, to release the oppressed, to proclaim the year of the Lord's favor. . . "Today this scripture is fulfilled in your hearing."
> —Luke 4:18-21

The basis for rescue from sin is Christ's conquest at the Cross.

This forms a summary of the ministry of Christ and what He is all about. The religious leaders missed it, and were incensed when He sought to reach tax collectors and sinners. The very human name of Jesus means *Jehovah's salvation*. It is in His character and name to rescue. When you cry out to God for rescue, you are calling upon God to do the very thing that is His delight. But how does He set imprisoned people free?

THE CROSS, THE BASIS FOR VICTORY

The basis for all rescue from sin is Christ's conquest at the cross. Not only is forgiveness of sin purchased, but when a person comes to faith in Christ, he is given a host of resources to enable him to be victorious against temptation, even over his greatest weakness. Before we came to faith, even though we had the ability to resist individual temptations, we had no supernatural power. Now, there is no limit to our resources, a fact stated in Ephesians 1:3:

> Praise be to the God and Father of our Lord Jesus Christ, who has blessed us in the heavenly realms with every spiritual blessing in Christ.
>
> —Ephesians 1:3

We must now avail ourselves of those resources. A part of learning a trade is learning the use of the tools of that profession. As believers we need to immerse ourselves in the Scriptures to learn the vast array of weapons at our disposal in conquering sin.

CONFESSION AND REBOUND

Facing our sin and helplessness is the starting point for God's rescue. Even in our greatest areas of disobedience God desires that we bring our repeated failure before Him in confession. Confession is an agreement with God.

John shows the importance of this agreement:

> If we claim to be without sin, we deceive ourselves . . . If we confess our sins, he is faithful and just and will forgive us our sins and purify us from all unrighteousness.
>
> —1 John 1:8-9

Some have used the illustration of a basketball backboard. A part of the game of basketball is grabbing the rebound from a missed shot, and heading the other direction. In confession, we agree with God that what we have done is wrong, and has injured God's reputation, others, and ourselves. After confession, we rebound; we yield our lives to God's power, and allow Him to live through us (see Galatians 2:20).

GOD'S WINDOW OF ESCAPE

Another fact of God's rescue is the way of escape provided for those tempted to sin. Let's call the way of escape a window of opportunity. In my experience, the window of escape gets larger or smaller based on the habits and choices we pursue. For those who have made bad choices repeatedly, the window may be very small. Here is how Paul states it:

> The window of escape gets larger or smaller based on the habits and choices we pursue.

No temptation has seized you except what is common to man. And God is faithful; he will not let you be tempted beyond what you can bear. But when you are tempted, he will also provide a way out so that you can stand up under it.

—1 Corinthians 10:13

You may say, "What about the addict? He has no choice!" We are all given an opportunity to obey God and make right choices. A drug addict met me in my office one day. He was a young man who knew Christ and yet had chosen drugs. Once he was settled in my office, he asked me to deliver him from his addiction. He wanted a magic bullet. I had to explain that just as he had narrowed the window of escape by saying, "Yes! Yes! Yes!" to drugs repeatedly, he could only make his escape easier by repeatedly saying, "No! No! No!" in the same area of temptation. God could enable him to do that. Though his life ended in a tragic accident, it seemed he was beginning a pattern of wiser choices.

LIVING DEATH, YET GRACE

As we have seen, Paul understood our struggle. Three times over a fourteen-year period, in desperate crises, he asked the Lord to remove a great trial from him. It seemed he could not go on. How much greater fruitfulness would come with his freedom? But the Lord's answer was a firm, "No!"

The vision he mentions may have occurred in a cave near Tarsus during Paul's seven to ten years of traveling evangelism and facing countless trials. After describing the visions he says:

> To keep me from becoming conceited because of these surpassingly great revelations, there was given me a thorn in my flesh, a messenger of Satan, to torment me. Three times I pleaded with the Lord to take it away from me. But he said to me, "My grace is sufficient for you, for my power is made perfect in weakness." Therefore I will boast all the more gladly about my weaknesses, so that Christ's power may rest on me. That is why, for Christ's sake, I delight in weaknesses, in insults, in hardships, in persecutions, in difficulties. For when I am weak, then I am strong.
> —2 Corinthians 12:7-10

What was his thorn in the flesh? Some have suggested eye trouble, headaches, physical results of his beatings, malaria, and epilepsy. And I want to suggest another: a strong area of temptation.

God Allows Thorns?

Notice in Paul's statement that God allowed the presence of this debilitating personal weakness, even though it was mediated through Satan, the enemy. Perhaps Paul or we would shake our fist in anger at our enemy for visiting this great struggle upon us.

> God allows nothing in the lives of His children that is not a part of His gracious dealing with us.

But remember that just as with Paul, God allows nothing in the lives of His children that is not a part of His gracious dealing with us, though we may not always know His specific reasons for allowing it.

As you read his description, notice the immensity of the trial this thorn represented to Paul. During the fourteen years he speaks of, it seems there were three points of crisis when he felt he could not possibly go on. Though he had endured multiple beatings, imprisonment, and shipwreck, these were nothing compared with the pain of this trial.

Paul's Conclusions and Ours

Let's look at some of Paul's conclusions in this life and death struggle with his greatest personal weakness that can also apply to our struggles:

- *It Bears Fruit.* For Paul, his struggle was a refiner's fire or forge that bore great fruit in his character and life for God. Is there any significant growth in our life apart from the thorns? We are brought into greater conformity to Christ through need, crisis, and frailty, as we are brought to depend on God alone.

- *It Produces Honesty.* When Paul says he would rather boast about his weaknesses, he has agreed 100 percent to God's assessment of them. No dodging, hiding, or disguising. Paul says that he is not ashamed to acknowledge them fully, to be completely honest about them, because it is God's plan for his glory to use the weak.

- *It Yields Contentedness.* What Paul says is revolutionary; he is actually content with weaknesses, distresses, and difficulties. The reason is that he has chosen to rest in God and His will, and live in the resources He provides, even in great struggle. We must also choose contentedness in God Himself instead of always looking for pleasant circumstances.

> I am not ashamed to acknowledge weaknesses fully, to be completely honest about them, because it is God's plan to use the weak for His glory.

- *It Trains Us.* Our human reasoning says strength is strength and weakness is weakness. We are flooded with sports broadcasts that analyze the weaknesses of players and teams. But Paul says, "When I am weak, then I am strong!" He has yielded to a strength beyond his own, which comes from God. He lives depending on God's resources instead of his own.

THE IMPACT OF VICTORY

I opened the chapter with the story of Dennis. In his long journey, he became honest about his struggle and began to say, "No!" to substances. Instead, he chose God's windows of escape.

He discovered a God who delivers the prisoner, and energizes for daily victory, through step-by-step choices. His victory has spread to touch countless lives, as he has since sponsored thousands of men in recovery programs.

God can use our greatest personal weaknesses to accomplish His glory and victory, and touch the world around us.

Think It Through

1. How does Dennis' struggle exemplify weaknesses we all face? What can the results be?

2. Why may feelings of spiritual defeat go beyond our actual spiritual failures?

3. How is the cross our basis for victory? How can one who has believed on Christ have forgiveness for daily sin?

4. Why did God allow the thorn to remain in Paul's life?

5. How have others benefited and God been glorified in your own struggle?

CHAPTER 10

WINNING THE DEATH
STRUGGLE WITH SELF

WE FACE A life or death struggle with sin and our sin nature.

In his forties, Glen emerged from twenty-plus years in prison, determined to begin a new life. His long list of crimes included the attempted murder of a police officer. He rented a room and took a job cleaning and doing maintenance for a church, but the well-meaning church fellowship was not aware of the strong lines of accountability needed to keep him productive and crime-free. Initially his failures included taking small amounts of money from desks. But after meeting someone in a bar, and repeated exposure to crack cocaine, he began a string of armed robberies. Convicted of a felony for the third and last time under California's three strikes law, Glen returned to prison.

> Individual sins are just the symptoms of the real disease, rebellion against God.

James, a gifted pastor, yielded to the temptation of internet pornography. When his failure was discovered, he left the ministry for secular employment. While attending my church he shared his ongoing struggle with me, but then moved away. The last time I heard from his family, he was in prison.

Eric fell into a pattern of continual unfaithfulness in his marriage. His wife kept their family together for the sake of the children, but Eric did not change.

Though our failures may differ in some respects, we all face a life and death struggle with sin. Individual sins are just the symptoms of the real disease—rebellion against God.

Sprinting Away from God

After four unhappy years in high school, I entered Chabot College, a local junior college, and felt liberated from prison. "Freedom at last!" I liked the courses I took and began to earn A's. At the same time, however, I joined the party crowd. They accepted me, and I entered into their round of beach trips, movies, and parties. Though their values were shallow and worldly, their love of life exhilarated me. My new life throbbed like the full volume beat of the juke box in the student union.

> I only have one life. I want to be happy. Is that so unreasonable?

My sprint away from God seemed justified by my conclusions: "God is determined to make me miserable, and force me to follow all His narrow rules!" "He makes people carry big Bibles, dress in second hand clothes, and go to Africa as missionaries." "He demands that His toadies shake their finger in people's faces and force them to repent." "He scowls at every small violation of His trivial rules that nobody can keep: *You didn't tie your shoes right this morning! I have got you again, you miserable rat!*

I wanted none of it and made excuses to soothe my conscience. *I only have one life. I want to be happy. Is that so unreasonable?*

Human happiness became my idol, and drove me away from a God I thought had imprisoned submissive fools in misery. I set a goal to become a millionaire after graduation from college. After all, I thought, *There's nothing money cannot buy!* I would amass my fortune in food franchises, like the two I had managed during college, and in real estate. A cousin had tripled his money in real estate on the California waterfront, and I thought I could duplicate his success. Satisfaction in life should be a slam dunk.

I never consulted God about my plans. I simply charted my own course. But a Bible verse I learned as a child tormented me: "For all have sinned and come short of the glory of God" (Romans 3:23 KJV). Still I squelched the voice of the Spirit in my quest for fulfillment.

I decided to stall any consideration of what God wanted for me until college ended. *We'll have a talk then,* I said. Who knows, I might even do my bit for God by giving a little time or money to some religious or humanitarian cause.

THE QUEST FOR HAPPINESS

In part, I longed to discover my place of significance, my place under the sun. Glory, fortune, and pleasure all seemed to beckon. The world screamed, *You have a right to happiness!* A wise mentor might have asked, *Where do you hope to find this fulfillment you seek?* I thought

My rebellion against God short-circuited discovering who I really was—my place of significance.

the answer was obvious: pursue whatever seemed pleasurable and appealing. My friends believed it, and they seemed living examples of giddy enjoyment. But my rebellion against God short-circuited discovering what I sought—my true identity.

Now, forty years later, I look back on my journey in college and realize I was not running toward happiness, but away from it. One never finds his place of greatness, and that is what God calls us to, apart from God's purpose. Yes, on our own we may discover some of our abilities and gifts, and our place in society, but our true and eternal significance can be found only in submission to God and His will.

> When Adam sinned, man received a bent to his nature . . . to do those things that harm himself, damage others, and dishonor God.

My misguided conclusions about God's motives could not have been more wrong. God is a good and loving parent who wants the best for each of His children. God designs and offers the best. I have grandchildren that may reject a nutritious meal, but long for the dessert of chocolate cake. But the parent or grandparent knows the child needs the good nutrition of the whole meal, and insists that it come first. I had rejected God and His will to seek the dessert of happiness.

THE BENT TO SIN

The talk show philosophy of today posits that man is basically good. But Scripture shows otherwise. When Adam sinned, man received a bent to his nature, and his tendency now is to sin, harm himself, damage others, and dishonor God. In this earthly life we cannot escape this inclination.

On long motor trips at night, I often get drowsy. When my wheels are out of alignment I have to keep a firm hand on the steering wheel to keep the car from drifting into another lane or off the road. In the same way, our bent to sin shows the misalignment of our hearts. If we are to stay on course in a life pleasing to God, *we must keep a steady hand on . . . habits and relationships* (Robert A. Pine, *Humanity & Sin*, Word).

Even Christ was tempted during His earthly life; Scripture says He was tempted in the very same manner we are. Evidence of the great struggle is seen in His temptation in the wilderness, and in His struggle in the Garden of Gethsemane. In both cases, so great was the conflict that afterward the Father sent angels to strengthen Him.

WILLING TO BE SEARCHED

Guilt is one of life's most painful emotions. It is excruciating when the Word of God and the Spirit of God point to our failure. It is humiliating when friends, family, or associates expose our sins, or reveal them to others. We feel demeaned, and struggle for equilibrium in overcoming anger, grief, or sorrow. But will we humble ourselves and allow the correction to purify, strengthen, and build us? For greatest health and wholeness, we must continually allow God's Spirit to search us—even when it is painful.

> For greatest health and wholeness, we must continually allow God's Spirit to search us—even when it is uncomfortable.

King Asa was one of the notable good kings of Judah, yet toward the end of his life, the prophet came to reprove him of a foolish decision to hire mercenaries to win a battle, instead of relying on the Lord. In his pride, the king justified himself, angrily rejecting correction. He was unwilling to acknowledge his failure, which might have necessitated the humiliating confession of his sin to God, the prophet, the leaders, and the people. In anger he added to his wrongs, imprisoned the prophet, and began to oppress some of the people.

> The believer not only has the ability to choose right, but . . . is given the supernatural power to do it.

We see the same tendency in the Pharisees of Christ's day; they chose to justify themselves at all cost—even to the point of crucifying the Savior. In contrast, we need to be open to correction so we can become people of genuine humility and submission before God.

CAN WE MASTER TEMPTATION?

In a tragic interplay in Genesis 4, Cain is moved to rage and murder by God's acceptance of his brother Abel's sacrifice instead of his own sacrifice. Abel's offering had been combined with an obedient heart. The Lord's words to Cain after the rejection of his gift are instructive:

> Then the LORD said to Cain, "Why are you angry? Why is your face downcast? If you do what is right, will you not be accepted? But if you do not do what is right, sin is crouching at your door; it desires to have you, but you must master it."
> —Genesis 4:6

Notice that although sin and failure were close, Cain still had an opportunity to master the temptation, and the Lord exhorted him to do so. He chose instead to murder his brother. The believer not only has the ability to choose right, but through the cross, the Spirit of God, and God's resources, he has the supernatural power to do it.

God's Payment for Our Sin

The concept of God's forgiveness is based in the fact that we have rebelled against God's law and character, and that rebellion is called sin. It is true of all of us as human beings (Romans 3:23). The penalty for sin is death, separation from God, even as declared to Adam and Eve (Genesis 2:17). During the Old Testament period, before Christ, the sin of repentant people was temporarily covered or atoned for through the Jewish Day of Atonement. When Christ came, He paid for all of man's sin at the cross, being the perfect sacrifice. He was a substitute for us, the guilty sinners before the court of God. And now through faith in Christ, we receive the miracle of complete forgiveness. We cannot earn it, but must rest completely on Christ and His full payment for us.

> Through faith in Christ, we receive the miracle of complete forgiveness.

Turning Around

Finally, at the end of college, I kept my promised appointment with God. At a 1965 college summer retreat we would have our little talk, then I would go my way and live the life I dreamed of. I registered for the retreat at Mount Hermon Conference Center in the Santa Cruz Mountains of California. When I turned to God, He shook me to my core, and my heart broke as I realized my sin of rebellion against Him. In tears of repentance I saw His love for me, and desire to direct my life. I vowed, "Lord, I will listen for the next step you have for me."

I returned to my college campus, looking for His guidance. He led me to a meeting of college students sponsored by Campus Crusade for Christ. The initial meeting was a jarring challenge to either serve God wholeheartedly, or give it up completely. No games, no pretense. It was the challenge I needed.

EXPERIMENT OF CONSECRATION

I walked home from that meeting deep in thought. As I passed the student union, I pictured myself wearing black, standing on a table with my Bible, shaking my finger at the miserable sinners, my fellow students. After all, that's what God requires, isn't it?

Though these misconceptions marred my thinking, I was convinced that God wanted all of me. Once home, I knelt beside an overstuffed chair and yielded my life to the Lord for one quarter of the school year. That was all the faith I had. *Lord, I will try it for one quarter. I will do whatever You want, and see what happens.*

That three-month term changed my life, as I began to read the Bible in the mornings, grow in faith, and seek God's plan for me. I also discovered all the little miracles God has in store for the person who will simply obey Him.

Having run from God, I now experienced the reality that in His infinite love, God pursues those who run. He longs to draw us to Himself in grace and forgiveness, no matter how far we have fled. It is never too late. And once we initiate the first steps to return, the Holy Spirit empowers us by His love and guidance to increasingly make the right choice.

Think It Through

1. Though we all battle with sin and the sin nature, why can it be characterized as a rebellion?

2. Why does disobedience to God change our theology or our view of God?

3. What voices around us tell us we have a right to happiness? If this is our supreme desire, why is it starting at the wrong place?

4. Why is it painful to be searched by the Word and Spirit of God? How did King Asa respond to that searching?

5. What is God's part in this great transformation of turning sinners to saints?

CHAPTER 11

EXCHANGING DAILY MISERY FOR JOY

AGAIN HEADED home from work with a scowl. Daily frustrations dogged me; work challenges I could not solve, and busy kids and home life that exhausted me. Often infuriated because I felt cheated of happiness, I reflected, "I am so miserable!"

Though my level of daily misery varied, every little thing fueled the volcano that was brewing inside of me. A visiting child broke a small limb off my apple tree, by accident, and it angered me. I arrived home to discover my children had been sliding on plastic on my front lawn. In response to my frustration, my wife responded, "You need to decide whether you want to raise kids or grass." I often pulled into the driveway only to launch into a tirade on what was wrong inside the house and out. Beverly wisely counseled, "You can't come home and immediately pronounce judgment on everything!"

> I am so miserable!

At other times, though my displeasure did not reach the level of anger, it clouded my thinking and behavior with vague discontent.

I evaluated everything in terms of what I wanted. At times I entered into long internal debates on the extent to which certain things or people pleased me.

LIFE'S INEVITABLE UPS AND DOWNS

Many of us live strapped to a roller coaster of circumstances. When adversity tips the status quo, we worry, fret, and feel cheated by life. When our fortunes are on the upswing, we assume it is what we deserve or we're filled with pride. Even Job, dealing with great adversity, felt abandoned by God. The opposite was true, but his thinking had been clouded by the pressure of adversity.

> Many of us live strapped to a roller coaster of circumstances.

> How I long for the months gone by, for the days when God watched over me, when his lamp shone upon my head and by his light I walked through darkness! Oh, for the days when I was in my prime, when God's intimate friendship blessed my house.
> —Job 29:2-4

At the end of his trial he saw reality; God was there all the time, guarding His beloved child.

When a teenager, I once rode the Santa Cruz, California roller coaster, the Big Dipper, seventeen times on the same day. Now, riding my feelings, I was once again king of the roller coaster.

"BE HAPPY!"

One reason we push so strenuously for giddy, personal pleasure is the model and message we see all around us. My battle corresponded to the world's philosophy: "The highest goal is to seek your own happiness and fulfillment. Your life is yours. You have the right, the responsibility to be happy. After all, what else is there?" You only live once, grab all the pleasure you can.

People are frantic to purchase a bigger HD television, a more luxurious boat, or a more expensive home as the obvious cure to their happiness void. Others rush to Las Vegas or purchase a sheaf of lottery tickets, grasping for the dream. Some immerse themselves in alcohol or substances, or rotate bedrooms and relationships. But these do not fill the yawning chasm. They never can; these "fulfillments" and others like them are far from the answers God provides for human fulfillment.

THE ALARM CLOCK

I could not see a way out of my unhappy state, until one moment when I felt the Lord prompting me, "Who is your god?"

"The Lord is my God!" I answered.

"No, your own happiness is your god. You will never find peace or your true place seeking to please yourself."

The insight stunned and saddened me. It stunned me because no matter what my professions, I had in practice been serving the wrong god—my own happiness. It saddened me because the Lord was my beloved, the one who loved me more deeply than I could fathom.

Your own happiness is your god!

It was then that the Lord impressed upon me, "I did not put you on earth to be happy, but to make Me happy, to please Me. You will only find your own happiness by living for Me!"

Was a self-serving God robbing me of every fragment of earthly pleasure? No: He was pointing me to the greatest pleasure man was created for. In my idolatry of my own pleasure, I had so focused on myself that I had missed the only true source of happiness—a love relationship with God Himself.

ROMANCE ANYONE?

God designed us for romance. Falling in love is one of the greatest joys of the human experience. When Beverly and I were dating, we took a car trip to Carlsbad Caverns in New Mexico. Freed temporarily from job and school, we enjoyed the natural wonder, the car trip, and being together. At one point as we approached the site, on a large grassy plain, we came to a railroad crossing. Since we saw no cars in any direction, we stopped at the crossing to kiss. It was with some embarrassment that a short while later we heard a car honk behind us. Another couple wanted to continue their journey, but our pause to do a little kissing was blocking their progress.

> Our greatest romance was designed to be with the Lord Himself.

Love brings an insatiable desire to get to know the other person, and to please him or her. You enjoy discovering each other's qualities, and increasingly sharing common interests together. There is a strong connection of mind, emotions, and will. Even the person's differences are intriguing.

OUR GREATEST RELATIONSHIP

Though marriage, parenting, and friendships are high priorities, our most important relationship is our romance with the Lord Himself, as reflected throughout the Scriptures. Enoch is said to have walked with God, the idea being that he must have pleased Him in every way (Genesis 5:21-24). The sons of Seth sought the Lord by calling on Him in prayer and perhaps sacrifice (Genesis 4:25-26). Noah was said to walk with God, and his life of obedience and integrity showed in his desire to please God (Genesis 6:8-9).

> Our romance with the Lord God is the solace for every relationship loss in life.

Moses found his joy in knowing God and drawing close to Him. At one point he longed to see all the Lord's glory and character. He said, "Now show me Your glory" (Exodus 33:18b).

RELATIONSHIP FAILURE

Perhaps your relationship experience has been heartbreak and loss through death, divorce, abandonment, or abuse. Or you may long for a relationship you have never found. Human relationships are always less than we idealize.

> Not only did God please us first, but He created us for the very purpose of pleasing Him.

Regardless of your personal situation, however, God is ready to be your friend, partner, lover, parent, spouse. He will never leave you or forsake you, as He promises in Scripture (Hebrews 13:5). He loves you personally, in infinite measure. No matter what your emptiness or loss, you still have your greatest romance. And your wounds can help draw you closer to this greater soul mate.

He Pleased Us First

In a romance, a supreme concern is seeking to please the other partner. Consider that in man's relationship with God, as seen in Genesis 1:27-31, He pleased us first. He initiated the love relationship. Immediately after creating man and woman, he blessed them. Consider other deep and powerful expressions of His love:

> This is love: not that we loved God, but that he loved us and sent his Son as an atoning sacrifice for our sins.
>
> —1 John 4:10

> We love because he first loved us.
>
> —1 John 4:19

Not only did God please us first, but He created us for the very purpose of pleasing Him.

> And we pray this in order that you may live a life worthy of the Lord and may please him in every way: bearing fruit in every good work, growing in the knowledge of God.
>
> —Colossians 1:10

> Finally, brothers, we instructed you how to live in order to please God, as in fact you are living. Now we ask you and urge you in the Lord Jesus to do this more and more.
>
> —1 Thessalonians 4:1

Man Turned Away from God: We Are the Runaway Bride

In contrast to the love relationship we are offered, consider that in our sin and rebellion we are the original runaway bride. Adam and Eve illustrate this tragic rejection and abandonment:

Then the man and his wife heard the sound of the LORD God as he was walking in the garden in the cool of the day, and they hid from the LORD God among the trees of the garden. But the LORD God called to the man, "Where are you?"

—Genesis 3:8-9

As sinners, flawed, sinful human beings, we have fled from God. In repentance and faith, we can return and be reconciled to the God we rejected. Then we can grow in our love relationship, living to please Him.

How Can We Please God?

Does God give us any guidance on how to please Him?

The shock of learning that I was living for my own happiness produced a longing to know what pleases God, to better orient my life toward Him. I began a study in the Scriptures, and found them awash with insights on how I could bring delight to God in my greatest love relationship. Here are a few of my discoveries:

- *Faith*—Unquestioned belief in God, His person and works, and what He has said. To place one's trust in Him, entrust oneself to Him, be faithful to Him. (Acts 16:31; Hebrews 11:6)
- *To Wait on Him*—Do His bidding, serve Him, be ready to do His will, wait upon Him as a servant, wait for Him—His timing and work. (Isaiah 40:31; Daniel 7:10)
- *To Know the Lord*—To know Him as a person, have personal dealings with Him. A growing understanding of His nature, will, and deeds. To grasp what distinguishes Him from all other beings. (Hosea 6:3, 6)

- *To Fellowship with Him*—Mutual sharing, the companionship and friendly association which God offers to men, always balanced with His sovereignty and Lordship. (Genesis 3:8; John 15:13-15)
- *To Walk with Him*—To accompany, walk continuously in fellowship with God, to follow a course of life that pleases Him. (Genesis 5:21-24)
- *To Delight in His Word*—To delight in God's Word is to delight in God's expression and declared will. (Psalm 119:14-15)
- *Believing Prayer*—Humble, sincere, earnest request made to God. Asking of God. (1 Thessalonians 5:16-18; Revelation 5:8)
- *To Live a Righteous Life*—Acting in a just, upright manner in conformity with God's commands. (Genesis 6:8-9)
- *Unity Among Believers in Christ*—Being of one spirit, esteeming and valuing each one. (Psalm 133)
- *Blameless Character*—To be free from fault or blame in one's pattern of behavior before others. (Psalm 15:1-5)
- *Humility, Brokenness before God*—Being humble, the absence of pride, one's will broken and submitted willingly to God. (Psalm 51:16-17; 57:15)
- *To Sacrifice, and Give the Greatest Sacrifice*—To give to God things that show the yielding of our inmost being to Him. (Romans 12:1-2)
- *To Delight in God*—To find supreme joy and pleasure in God Himself, apart from His gifts. (Psalm 22:8)
- *Worship*—Acts of devotion to God, throughout life, that demonstrate His worth. (Hebrews 13:15; Ephesians 5:18-20)
- *Compassion*—A growing awareness of the calamity and pain of others, and actions to alleviate it. (Isaiah 11:16-17; Hebrews 13:16)

I also discovered that I could learn much about what pleases God from many other parts of Scripture:

- Summaries of what pleases God, e.g. Micah 6:8
- Summaries of what displeases God, e.g. Proverbs 6:16-19
- Examples of character and deeds that please God, e.g. Genesis 6:9, 22
- Examples of things that displease God, e.g. Acts 5:1-4

As you can guess, I discovered that the supreme example of what pleases the Father is seen in Jesus, the Son of God.

UNITED WITH THE BELOVED

My discoveries seemed a small turn in the right direction, but they inspired me to pay more attention to my motives and actions. And they inspired a new purpose to please God instead of myself. My daily misery slowly began to ebb. It also enhanced my relationship with others, as I no longer treated them as servants of my own happiness. My joy in living began to grow as I redirected my focus away from myself and toward God.

I began to live in the richness of God's love, as I discovered one can never out love God. In a thousand ways He seeks to please those who seek to please Him. He joys in our joy, and we increasingly live in the pleasure of His smile.

Think It Through

1. Are you strapped to the roller coaster of circumstances? How has that impacted your life and the lives of those around you?

2. How does the world encourage us to deify our own happiness and pleasure?

3. For whose pleasure are we called to live? What does that have to do with our relationship with God?

4. How can your relationship with God be a solace in disappointing human relationships?

5. In what senses did God please us first?

EXTERNALS THAT FRUSTRATE US

CHAPTER 12

SOLVING LIFE'S PUZZLES

EXHAUSTED FROM A demanding seminary routine, on a cold Friday Beverly and I bundled our two-year-old and five-month-old into our small sedan. We would trek 300 miles from Dallas, Texas, to Odessa for Christmas with Beverly's family. Somewhere after we passed Fort Worth, large white clumps of snow began to clobber our windshield.

It was accumulating fast. Suddenly an explosion in the engine compartment signaled trouble, and the car began losing power. Seeking an exit, we pulled off the freeway into a small crossroads with a gas station and a motel.

"Just great!" I fumed. "We're exhausted, broke, and now we have huge car problems. Life is impossible!"

> We're exhausted, broke, the weather is abysmal, and now we have huge car problems. Life is just impossible!

Frustration with seemingly hopeless situations was not new. Throughout my childhood and young adult years I often felt overwhelmed by challenges. The feeling surfaced again in adult life at times of adversity and anxiety. I had always felt out of step with others, like a bystander, lacking any real friends and without a sense of accomplishment. Everyone else seemed to know who they were and what they were doing, while I felt blocked and lost.

THE WORLD OF IMPOSSIBLES

Perhaps, like me, you find life frustrating. We all have mountains to climb. In my circle of family and friends right now there is job loss, mental illness, death, divorce, poor moral choices, a losing battle with cancer, and attempted suicide.

> Mountains can be handled. Changing people, however, is another story. They are the more stubborn mountains.

Though we face multiple problems, perhaps relationships are the single greatest challenge. I have a friend who served as a colonel with the National Guard near Seattle, Washington. He reminded people that moving Mt. Ranier, the greatest feature of the Seattle skyline, was just a matter of earthmoving equipment, manpower, and time. Mountains can be handled. Changing people, however, is another story. They are the more stubborn mountains.

Lynn, for example, battled with a difficult relationship. As a girl, her dad, a busy Ph.D. and professor, had limited time for his daughter. His lack of affection left a hole in Lynn's life. Her parents also had high standards, and she felt demeaned by statements such as, "You will never play the piano as well as your sister." "You will always be a quitter."

Always Climbing, Never Summiting

I had a boss who, facing the frustrations of the business environment, reminded me of a story in Greek mythology. Sisyphus was sentenced to roll a huge rock to the top of a hill, but each time he reached the top, the stone rolled back down. Many of us feel like this frustrated mythological character.

In some cases, the result of constant impossibilities can be fatal. Jim battled waves of guilt and shame over his addiction, and took his own life. Les, battling years of pain from a work injury, attempted suicide by jumping off a bridge.

More often, impossibilities leave us feeling thwarted. As a child, I was often frustrated by puzzles and things I could not solve. I would give up and vent my anger. In adult life, discouragement often caused me to point a finger of blame at others. At times I spent sleepless nights inflamed with anger until God illuminated the flaws in my own behavior and attitude. At other times frustrations caused me to point inwardly, and blame myself despite the fact that the Lord had not convicted me of such responsibility.

Anxiety often results when we feel thwarted in attaining our goals, encounter adversity, or battle imaginary, inward conflicts. Anxiety can also be the product of moral anguish concerning our own perceived failures.

Why does God allow his children to face frustrating circumstances such as family conflict, opposition on the job, and business failure? Can't He make the mountains disappear, or at least reduce them to manageable size? Can't He make us stronger so we can face the challenges?

Why Impossibilities?

At the end of the forty years in the wilderness, the Lord commented on the benefit of the long period of testing the Israelites endured:

Remember how the LORD your God led you all the way in the desert these forty years, to humble you and to test you in order to know what was in your heart, whether or not you would keep his commands. He humbled you, causing you to hunger and then feeding you with manna, which neither you nor your fathers had known, to teach you that man does not live on bread alone but on every word that comes from the mouth of the LORD. Your clothes did not wear out and your feet did not swell during these forty years. Know then in your heart that as a man disciplines his son, so the LORD your God disciplines you.

—Deuteronomy 8:2-5

On the surface, the time in the desert was long and frustrating. But God paused to give them insight into the actual benefits they received from their day-to-day adventure in adversity. Physical hunger prepared them to see God's miraculous, supernatural provision of manna. In all their needs He taught them to depend on Him alone, to receive His supply, and praise Him for it. The Lord called the process discipline. As a parent trains a child, God shaped the children of Israel for their maturity and benefit.

MOUNTAIN CLIMBING RESOURCES

God has perfectly equipped us for the daily frustrations of life.

I have some experience climbing the peaks in Yosemite National Park. Several times I have hiked Mt. Dana (13,061 feet) and a dozen times I have climbed Half Dome. Critical to any attempt is equipment. Poorly equipped, I spent one miserable night at 12,000 feet in brutal cold and wind when attempting a 14,000 foot peak. My sleeping bag and tent were inadequate and I suffered greatly.

I have better news for you. God has perfectly equipped us for the daily frustrations of life. Though suffering is a reality for all of us, He provides what we need, when we need it:

- God strengthens and enables us to do everything that is in His will for us. He works through our limited human abilities, infusing us with His strength: "I can do everything through Him who gives me strength" (Philippians 4:13).
- We can give thanks in everything because God is working His perfect purpose in all. "Always giving thanks to God the Father for everything, in the name of our Lord Jesus Christ" (Ephesians 5:20).
- We can have peace of mind as we yield every issue to God. "Do not be anxious about anything, but in everything, by prayer and petition, with thanksgiving . . . and the peace of God . . . will guard your hearts and minds in Christ Jesus" (Philippians 4:6-7).
- All is under His lordship. ". . . and put everything under his feet. In putting everything under him, God left nothing that is not subject to him. Yet at present we do not see everything subject to him" (Hebrews 2:8).
- We are given supernatural, inward resources for every need. They enable us to respond in Christlike character. "May the God of peace . . . equip you with everything good for doing his will . . ." (Hebrews 13:20-21).

Lord, It's Just Impossible

The disciples faced a puzzling impossibility on one occasion (Mark 6:32-44). The Lord had taken them by boat to a private place for a needed rest. But the public clamor for Christ's ministry led the crowds to follow. Christ, in his compassion, seized the opportunity, healed and taught, but as evening approached there were no means to feed the multitude. The disciples suggested Jesus send the crowds away to find food for themselves. In response, Christ gave a startling command: "They do not need to go away. You give them something to eat!"

> Doing what God gives you to do, and allowing Him to do what only He can do is the key to solving the impossible.

Why would the Savior, who loved them, say such a thing, when He knew they had no adequate resources? Was He mocking their lack or inability? No, He was just providing another learning opportunity to show how God provides what is needed to flawed human beings with limited resources. He could easily create the needed food Himself, but instead Jesus gave them the key to solving all of life's challenges.

- *They Evaluated Their Resources.* In response to Christ's startling command, the disciples found it would take eight months wages to buy a little food for each person (Mark 6:37; John 6:7). They informed the Savior that they had five loaves and two fish—a ridiculous quantity compared with the need. Many times we stop here facing insurmountable needs, dissolving in unbelief.
- *They Realized Their Inability.* Truly Jesus was asking the impossible. In order for them to see the immensity of the task, they had to see that it was not only beyond their resources, but beyond their ability. Even if they could bankroll the project, which they could not, supplies would be inadequate for the purchase. The lack prepared them to evaluate the size of the miracle about to occur.

- *They Did What God Gave Them to Do.* Do not miss the fact that the disciples had a part in the miracle. Jesus multiplied the loaves and fish, but He had them measure the resources, and seat and count the crowd. Though weak in faith, He had work for them to do. But when they had performed all He asked them to do, they had to look to the Savior to do the rest.
- *They Looked to God to Do What Only God Could Do.* Doing what God gives you to do, and allowing Him to do what only He can do is the key to solving the impossible.

Often we want our solution to obstacles, not what God purposes to bring. And how many times do we take on our human shoulders what can only be accomplished by God?

Earlier, I talked about my family's Christmas trip when the children were young. I was upset with my impossible situation, the car, the weather, and everything else.

Immersed in despair, I nevertheless asked the mechanic to look at the engine and confirm our desperate situation. "It's only a blown spark plug," he said. "One of your plugs was loose, and blew right out of the socket. That was the bang you heard. All you need is an eighteen-cent replacement and you will be on your way."

As we pulled out of the station, my embarrassment belied guilt at my frustration due to unbelief. Those who follow Jesus Christ are to expect the impossible. The Lord reminds us in Scripture that we will face challenges that will test us to the core. But we can take heart; our God has overcome the world. We need only do what He asks of us, and allow Him to do what only He can do.

When facing our deepest challenges we can say, "Thank You, Lord; it's just another impossible. I will step out to do my part. Glorify Yourself by doing what only You can do."

Think It Through

1. Which of your challenges seem most impossible to solve?

2. Why does God allow us to face frustrating circumstances?

3. Facing a huge, hungry crowd, how did Christ help the disciples evaluate the human impossibility of the situation? (Mark 6:32-44)

4. What part did the disciples have in the miracle?

5. What was God's part in the miracle?

CHAPTER 13

UNLOCKING PURPOSE IN SUFFERING

MIDDAY, A KNOCK sounded on Lloyd's front door. "Lloyd, you better sit down, there has been a tragedy in Steve's family." Stephen was his thirty-seven-year-old son. "Stephen has drowned in the Smith River, rescuing his daughter Kacia. She is fine, but Stephen lost his life."

Overwhelmed by grief Lloyd says, "I felt like I had a literal hole in my heart. Whenever I drove over a bridge I pictured Steven drowning. After seventy-five days I went to his grave, and took some photos of him. I cried my eyes out. I then wrote out seven pages of memories of his life."

> After seventy-five days
> I went to his grave . . .
> I cried my eyes out.

ALL SUFFER

We all experience suffering. The classic schoolroom of suffering in the Scriptures is the Book of Job. Described as the wealthiest man of the East, Job becomes the object of a contest between God and

Satan. At a time in heaven when the angels came before Him, the Lord asks Satan, "Have you considered my servant Job? There is no one on earth like him; he is blameless and upright, a man who fears God and shuns evil" (Job 1:8b). Satan claims that Job only serves the Lord for the blessings and protection He bestows. In two phases the Lord allows Satan to test Job; to inflict suffering on his faithful servant to determine the issue. Job is left bereft of his children and his property, covered with boils, sitting in ashes. His flesh became encrusted with dirt, oozing, covered with worms. Satan inflicted the greatest suffering he could to tempt him to curse God.

Why Has Suffering Come?

What then ensued was a debate between Job and his friends about the reasons for his suffering. Eliphaz, the first friend or comforter to make a statement, says, "Consider now, who being innocent has ever perished? Where were the upright ever destroyed?" (Job 4:7). He assumed Job's suffering was because of sin, and that God was reproving him severely. It was a quick, judgmental conclusion that all of us tend to draw when we view one in adversity. Sadly, it is usually ignorant of the real facts.

> The innocent or righteous sometimes suffer.

One of the things Job's friends missed, and one of the great lessons of the book, is that the innocent or righteous sometimes suffer. Their pain is not for their own sins, but due to other causes, and Job is a case in point. Though he is a righteous man of character, and one who compassionately cares for others, because of Satan's desire to dishonor God, suffering has come. The classic case of an innocent sufferer is Jesus, in 1 Peter 2:18-25:

Christ suffered for you, leaving you an example, that you should
follow in his steps.

"He committed no sin, and no deceit was found in his mouth."

—1 Peter 2:21b-22

EVALUATING OUR PAIN

In suffering, how should we handle our pain? I have found
that a distressing tendency in my own life is to bury it or deny it.
At times I seek to carry on, despite the pain, crippled by wounds.
I have discovered that we serve
a God of truth who wants us to
be people of the truth. A great
psychologist and physician has
said, "Let the deep pain hurt."
Because we need to face the truth,
and live in truth, it is valuable to not only realize the fact of our
pain, but to evaluate the depth of our pain. The tendency may be
to say, "What good will that do? I cannot change my situation." But
in a moment we want to examine some responses to pain.

Let the deep pain hurt.

REASONS FOR SUFFERING

After grappling with the reality of our suffering, and its depth,
we need to discern its cause. Often it will not be a single source,
and we will need to discover the various reasons for our anguish.
But because we cannot claim that all our suffering is without cause,
let's investigate some of the sources of suffering:

1. Yes, some suffering is because of *sin*. Peter exhorts us:

    If you suffer, it should not be as a murderer or thief or any other
    kind of criminal, or even as a meddler.

    —1 Peter 4:15

2. Related to the above, when those who know the Lord sin, *God reproves them*, and that reproof may be through adversity.

> My son, do not make light of the Lord's discipline, and do not lose heart when he rebukes you, because the Lord disciplines those he loves, and he punishes everyone he accepts as a son.
>
> —Hebrews 12:5b-6

3. Some suffering arrives because we have a *spiritual enemy* that seeks to harm us, defeat us, and block us from fulfilling the high purpose God has for each life.

> So Satan went out from the presence of the LORD and afflicted Job with painful sores from the soles of his feet to the top of his head.
>
> —Job 2:7

But, like Job, it is difficult to know what specific elements of our suffering have come from the enemy.

4. Some affliction comes from our *fellow human beings*. For Job, the Sabeans and Chaldeans were the source of some of his anguish (Job 1:15, 17). Though moved or incited by Satan, they are still responsible for their bloodshed and theft.
   Another source of suffering is the *calamity that comes to all:*

> He causes his sun to rise on the evil and the good, and sends rain on the righteous and the unrighteous.
>
> —Matthew 5:45b

> Shall we accept good from God, and not trouble?
>
> —Job 2:10b

Though a frustrating part of life, this source of affliction is a part of human existence, and cannot be blamed to sin, Satan, or the evil of others.

WHERE DO I TURN?

Where do we go in our pain? Our tendency is to use every fiber of our being to immediately solve our situation, and remove the suffering. But often, that is not an option, as it was not an option for Job.

- *Cry out to God in prayer*, as David does in Psalm 57:

Have mercy on me, O God, have mercy on me, for in you my soul takes refuge. I will take refuge in the shadow of your wings until the disaster has passed.

—Psalm 57:1

The tendency may be to say, "What good will that do?" But prayer opens up the comfort of connection to God in the most powerful relationship available to us. Express yourself to God in brutal frankness, not only about the facts, but about your feelings.

> Prayer plugs us in to the most powerful realm of accomplishment.

- *Ask concrete things of God* connected to your situation and feelings. In the lament Psalms, the largest classification of Psalms, there is always a petition, specific requests asked of God. I tend to complain and whine without asking. But prayer plugs us in to the most powerful realm of accomplishment and changes our situation.

- *Share your adversity and pain with others.* In their most helpful action, Job's friends listened for seven days before ever speaking (Job. 2:13). Often because of our pain, we may want to isolate ourselves, but healing starts as we share our anguish with compassionate listeners. Often they can share wisdom, and their companionship is a presence that warms and heals.
- *Seek and accept God's comfort.* Even if reproved by God, there is comfort in His Fathering care. It is His beloved sons and daughters He corrects.

Praise be to the God and Father of our Lord Jesus Christ, the Father of compassion and the God of all comfort, who comforts us in all our troubles . . . .
—1 Corinthians 1:3-4a

A wonderful healing resource is to spend much time in His Word, the Bible. During times of suffering, I have found the Psalms a bottomless source of comfort.

- *Give comfort, help, and healing to others.* Your immediate reaction to this suggestion may be: "Wait a minute; I thought we were talking about *my* pain!" But in pain I have often found the greatest salve in giving to others, and reaching outside of myself. The most effective person to minister to the suffering of others is one in pain.

- *Entrust yourself and your anguish to God.*

So then, those who suffer according to God's will should commit themselves to their faithful Creator and continue to do good.
—1 Peter 4:19

This was the response that Jesus Himself took:

When they hurled their insults at him, he did not retaliate; when he suffered, he made no threats. Instead, he entrusted himself to him who judges justly.

—1 Peter 2:23

This type of trust means that instead of solving the situation ourselves, we give ourselves to God, His solution, and His infinite power and wisdom, and yield to be obedient to what He directs.

- *Determine to endure,* to persevere in a manner pleasing to God, with good character, avoiding pitfalls such as revenge or despair.
- *Turn to God in praise.* Even in the deepest cries and laments in the Psalms, the writer invariably turns to trust in God and praise, exalting God. We can determine where we set our thoughts, and can purposely turn from the negative. It is not all about us, but about God. In the darkest moments of suffering and loss I have never been closer to my glorious God, and turned to Him in praise.

Conclusions about Suffering

Since we have looked to Job as one of our teachers, let me use that insightful book to draw some insights into suffering. Here I am in debt to D. A. Carson in his classic *How Long, O Lord.*

1. Suffering falls within the cover of God's sovereignty. The source of suffering was Satan's desire to dishonor God by forcing Job to curse God. But Satan's afflictions could only come as allowed by God.

2. Bigger issues are at stake than Job's comfort, or physical or mental welfare. Though he did not know it, Job was on display. We do not understand all the ways God is using our suffering.

3. There is such a thing as innocent or righteous suffering. Job seemed to maintain a deep conviction of his approval before God's eyes that carried him through the trial.

4. What Job feared most had come upon him (Job 3:25). God often must bring what we fear the most to deliver us from false gods, and nurture yieldedness to Him alone.

5. God does not blame us if, in our suffering, we vent our frustration. Of course we can say wrong things and blasphemous things, which we must try to avoid (Job 2:9). Though Job's lament seems shocking, in the end God affirmed that Job said what was right (Job 42:7).

> Mystery surrounds many of the reasons and details encompassing suffering.

6. Mystery surrounds many of the reasons and details encompassing suffering. Job found this deeply troubling. Part of his anguish is that the reason for his suffering is hidden (Job 3:23).

7. Job did not abandon faith in God. Though he had lost almost everything else, he clung firmly to his hope in God, and so must we.

GOD, THE GREAT SUFFERER

Perhaps in our pain we would be tempted to shake our fist to heaven and say, "What do You know about suffering, sitting in Your heavenly bliss!" But the reality is God *is* the Great Sufferer, the Infinite Suffer. Consider that all sin is rebellion against the God who loves us; it is a personal wound, a galling rejection. We see the Father giving His Son to die, and the Son giving Himself in death though it meant the most tragic separation theology can fathom: "My God, My God, Why hast thou forsaken me?" (Mark 15:34b).

On Display

In a study of 1 Peter, we discover that in suffering God is often putting his anguished servant on *display* before others. This may not be entirely comfortable at a time of personal struggle. But as we live lives of character, though tested, God declares Himself, His character, and His provision for people who suffer.

Giving Birth in Suffering

Recently, I suffered with comments critical of my ministry. As I struggled for equilibrium, I was also planning a training session for a struggling ministry that needed volunteers. In my pain, I began telephoning, and to my surprise something began to happen. The almost universal response was, "Yes, I would like to come. I have been thinking about getting involved." The result was a miracle, a packed training meeting, and a new beginning for a ministry. It

> God gives birth to many things through human pain.

reminded me again that God gives birth to many things through human pain. Perhaps in every experience of suffering we should ask, "Lord, how do You want to use this to bring forth something great?"

SUFFERING RESULTS IN GLORY

The blessing God brings through suffering is not just for the present. In his discussion of trials, Peter says:

> These have come so that your faith—of greater worth than gold, which perishes even though refined by fire—may be proved genuine and may result in praise, glory and honor when Jesus Christ is revealed.
>
> —1 Peter 1:7

Though it is hard to see through our tears, there is a greater and eternal glory, and God is working through our pain. He is still working His perfect good in our lives, bringing a model and message to those around us, and bringing glory to His own name.

Lloyd suffered in the death of his son, Steven. But after grieving at the cemetery, the Lord began using Steven's death to heal others. "When I left his grave that night, the deep, deep hurt was gone . . . I didn't choose my [tragedy], but I had to seize it for Jesus Christ. The tragedy brought me to people I would never have had the pleasure of meeting or the privilege of sharing Jesus Christ with in any other way. I had two choices: I could either be bitter at God or better for Him.

Think It Through

1. What have been your most painful experiences of suffering?

2. Considering both the human and spiritual realms; what are some causes of suffering?

3. Where should we turn while suffering? What sources of solace have been most helpful to you?

4. In what sense is God the Great Sufferer?

5. What does it mean to give birth in suffering? Why would someone say, "Don't waste your pain!"?

CHAPTER 14

DEMOLISHING THE SHAME OF MOCKERY

THE OVERPASS

THE TEN OF us mocked his appearance. We surrounded a quiet seven-year-old boy with a red birthmark on his face. As if slinging fist-sized mud balls full-force, we hurled insults, laughing at this boy we considered a freak, a loser. We were "normal" and proud of it.

The scene by the overpass is burned into my memory. I still live where I grew up and am reminded whenever I see it. I will never forget the scene, not only because it marked the victim, but because it also marked me with the stain of guilt and sorrow.

> Sticks and stones may break my bones.

WORDS HURT

Have you ever mocked someone? Have you ever been mocked? We've all heard the saying, Sticks and stones may break my bones, but words will never hurt me! Though a popular saying amongst children, words do hurt. And words are only a slender, seven per cent of communication. Facial expression, tone of voice, and body language are the more devastatingly significant parts of communication.

Most mocking does not take place to a person's face, but behind his back with backbiting and gossip. After all, the person can't see it or hear it, so what's the harm? And it feels so good to tear down another. *What he doesn't know won't hurt him!*

The impact can be shame, smallness, embarrassment, guilt, and despair. The impact may be more than immediate, but lifelong, devastating a person's sense of his place under God's sun.

You Are in Good Company

If you have suffered the sting of mocking, you are in good company. Christ suffered under cruel jeers in His arrest and crucifixion (Matthew 27:28-31; 39-44), when He was mocked as a supposed king, a sham, a no-account play actor. Christ patiently bore the abuse, secure in His identity and in the Father's plan. Job was verbally belittled by those younger and of less character, and some of them spat on him in his degraded state (Job 30:1, 8-10). Hannah, the mother of Samuel, was bitterly ridiculed by Elkanah's second wife (1 Samuel 1:3-8). Mocking was also one of the trials commonly endured by the saints of old (Hebrews 11:32-38).

Demeaning attacks always take an emotional and physical toll on the one attacked. When Christ was tempted and belittled by Satan in the wilderness, he was already depleted by fasting. In love toward His Son, the Father sent an angel to strengthen and encourage Him (Matthew 4:1-11).

I Was Only Kidding!

There are those who defend mocking with convenient retorts:

"Can't you take a joke? I was only kidding."

"Where's your sense of humor?"

"We were laughing with you, not at you!"

"Don't be so thin-skinned."

"What's the matter, can't you laugh at yourself?"

God is seen laughing in Psalm 2:4, when the nations plot against Him. Having a sense of humor is a part of our emotional and psychological makeup. But mocking is not just humor; it is assaulting another human being with words, actions, attitude, and body language. Does laughing at our mutual faults ever have a place? Possibly, if it is done in a framework of love and acceptance, without being demeaned or shamed.

> "We were laughing with you, not at you!"

While living in the Philippines with the military, Beverly and I often served home cooking to American service personnel with roast beef, potatoes, and homemade pie. As veterans of chow hall fare, our guests ate ravenously. None was embarrassed to ask for seconds or thirds. But we discovered another kind of "roast" served up at the table. The men filled the meal time with little comments about each other's appearance, nationality, or idiosyncrasies. Often a man left wounded in spirit. For many of us, mocking has become a regular and permissible part of life.

How God Feels about Mocking

When the Lord lists seven things that He hates in Proverbs 6:16-19, the first on the list is a proud look (KJV), or haughty eyes

(NASB). In our world, an arrogant look is constant fare, and is a close associate of mocking. Why would God pick such a seemingly small thing to headline the list of things He hates? Because it destroys His fragile creatures, inflates pride, and dishonors God who created man in His image.

A slant on arrogance is the child or youth that mocks his parents. Proverbs shows God's displeasure and reproof of this dishonoring:

> The eye that mocketh at his father, and despiseth to obey his mother, the ravens of the valley shall pick it out, and the young eagles shall eat it.
>
> —Proverbs 30:17 (KJV)

WHAT IS MOCKING?

Here are some insights into the meaning of mocking:

- *It is a lie.* It evaluates a person by temporary human measure and declares a person's low worth, contrary to God's verdict. (Acts 17:32)
- *It is slander,* an insult and a slur, whether to their face or behind their back. (See Matthew 27:39-44)
- *It dishonors God's creation,* demeans, marginalizes. God says He has created each person unique and perfect according to His plan, and worthy of honor (Psalm 139:13-15). He admonishes us to honor everyone (1 Peter 2:17).
- *It also dishonors God* because He has created us in His image (Genesis 1:26-27).
- *It judges a person* and his worth with no authority to do so (James 4:11-12).
- *It destroys the spirit* of a person and vandalizes a person's emotional and psychological worth (Luke 22:63-65).
- *It is a personal rejection* (Mark 10:33-34).

THE DAMAGE

In speaking about the damage inflicted by mocking, Frank Peretti, in *The Wounded Spirit*, sounds a prophetic voice. Growing up with a medical condition that left him disfigured, he was cruelly mocked and abused as a child. He wrote:

> At the time of this writing, I'm close to fifty years of age, but I still remember the names and can see the faces of those individuals who made my life a living hell, day after day after day, during my childhood. I remember their words, their taunts, their blows, their spittle, and their humiliations.

> You've been wounded in your spirit, and that wound pierces deeply, painfully, sometimes even permanently. As Proverbs 18:14 says, "The spirit of a man will sustain him in sickness, but who can bear a broken spirit?" When tough times or injuries come, we must be able to draw upon a reservoir of hope, faith, and self-confidence that God has stored up inside us through the love and encouragement of friends and family. If enemies, through cunning and cruelty, have plundered that reservoir, what will sustain us then?

THE SCRIPT

In drama, the actors are handed scripts depicting the person they are to play. Just like actors, we enter into life every day with a mental script of who we are, of our worth, our roles, and whether or not we are loved or valued. It gives us a sense of our place and what we can reasonably be expected to accomplish. Part of the power of mockery is that it sends us into the drama of life with a script that has been devastatingly mutilated. Instead of seeing ourselves under God as unique and significant people, we often believe the damaged script handed to us.

I am in contact with a family where a thirteen-year-old boy was recently told by a family member that he was a mistake.

I TELL IT LIKE IT IS

If you are a mocker, you may feel truth is your justification. "I tell it like it is!" "I am a straight shooter." "I don't beat around the bush!" Is truth really your motivation? No one possesses all truth, nor can anyone perfectly balance the truth he thinks he has with other truths. Your evaluation of "He's a loser!" or "What an idiot!" is a temporary evaluation based on surface and rapidly changing values. This is exactly the kind of judging Scripture warns against. The Lord described the vast difference between man's flawed evaluation and God's measure when the sons of Jesse were being evaluated for the call to be king.

> But the LORD said to Samuel, "Do not look at his appearance or at the height of his stature, because I have rejected him; for God sees not as man sees, for man looks at the outward appearance, but the LORD looks at the heart."
>
> —1 Samuel 16:7 (NASB)

Even godly Samuel, on this occasion, would have chosen wrongly based on human evaluation. Surface conclusions are misleading.

The truth we do have can be used to build others up, by speaking the truth in love, face-to-face (Ephesians 4:15a).

CHRIST'S WORDS AND EXAMPLE

Verbally demeaning another may be what Christ spoke of in the following verse:

. . . but whosoever shall say, Thou fool, shall be in danger of
hell fire.

—Matthew 5:22b (KJV)

Calling someone a fool (Aramaic *raca*) is declaring they are
empty, worthless, or insane, worthy of being demeaned as a person
and unworthy of honor. The Lord shows that no one should be
dishonored in this way, even the mentally disabled. The Lord
considers this failure so serious, there is a danger of extreme
punishment. (Gehenna, the Valley of Hinnom, is a figure for divine
punishment.)

Who is in a greater one-up position to mock than God Himself?
Though Christ was jeered, because of His measureless love for
men, He honored rather than demeaned people. He treated the
Samaritan woman with respect (John 4), though she was despised
by the Jews, and possibly by her own people as well. He received
lepers and healed them (see Matthew 8:2-4). He conveyed honor
to despised Gentiles, the Syrophoenician woman (Mark 7:25-30),
and the Centurian (Matthew 8:5-11), because of their great faith.
He won Zaccheaus to faith, a hated tax collector, and dined with
him in his home (Luke 19:1-10).

GETTING UP FROM THE MAT

If you are reeling from being mocked, you may have to
acknowledge feelings of shame, humiliation, smallness, and grief.
Emotions are a part of our human nature and we are vulnerable
to the opinions of others. Demeaning evaluations wound us. We
care what others think of us. We want to be liked, loved, admired,
the object of a good opinion. But remember, in the end it is what
God thinks of us that counts. Only He can see perfectly the heart
of a person, and this is the center of His evaluation.

God Encourages and Builds Up

Just as others may have purposely demeaned you, God much more strongly affirms you. Though as ones who have rebelled against Him, we need His salvation; God values and treasures humans that He has created in His image. Bask in God's personal love and care for you as you trade the script of the mocked for the script of one loved and valued infinitely. Immerse yourself in Scriptures that show He views you as His glorious and perfect creation. Treasure your assets and see your true worth. Refresh yourself in your high call under God. Tell yourself, *My worth rests in God, who has created me perfect according to His plan, and showed His love for me by redeeming me with the death of His Son.*

Set a Plan to Move Forward

Though revenge may seem sweet, fight the tendency to take it. It is human to want to strike back, but biblical examples, including Christ, show the better course: leaving revenge to God. God is well able to defend His own.

If you have been wounded in the fabric of human relationships don't isolate yourself; instead yield to healing bonds with others. If you are fearful or suspicious because of past hurts, I exhort you to learn new skills in initiating friendship (Proverbs 18:24 KJV). You will be nourished in many ways, enabling you to get your eyes off yourself.

Into the Garden of Gethsemane, one of the darkest moments of His human life, Christ gathered His friends, the disciples. He shared His moment of deepest agony, and asked them to pray for Him.

A Redemptive Perspective

Form a redemptive perspective of those who demean you. Christ's plan was to heal the very ones who mocked Him. They cried, "Crucify him!" Christ answered, "Father, forgive them, for they do not know what they are doing" (Luke 23:34b). The *them* refers to everyone involved in the monstrous injustice of the cross, including the mockers. In return for injury, He purposed to give healing and life.

God will enable you to turn the tables, to heal those who wound you as you grow in His love. Though our mockers have exercised power over us, through the power of God we can help heal those who have injured us.

Deliver Your Case to God

Among the Laments, the cries of distress in the Psalms, there are some called *Imprecatory Psalms*. The most extreme seem to call down God's judgment on the writer's enemies, and some biblical authorities consider them invalid expressions for the New Testament believer. I see them as delivering a legal case to the Great Judge, pleading a cause in detail before God's throne. It is the supreme resource of the weak, the abused, and the wronged. We should bring the greatest injustices of life to God's throne when we have been wronged. Deliver to Him the offense, tell Him how galling it is, how you feel about it, how it has harmed others, and how it has dishonored Him.

You cannot avoid being mocked or dishonored. Those who carry the cross of Jesus will suffer in this life. But the Savior shows that the one mocked can know true triumph, in the enabling of Christ, the supreme Victor.

The Victor

Frank Pieretti, in his volume *The Wounded Spirit*, exposed the reality and results of mocking. His book was an 8.0 earthquake to many who had assumed mocking was a victimless crime. He was interviewed repeatedly by James Dobson, and his book began to reshape our perspective of the damage done by mocking. He rose above his wounds to heal both the mocked and the mocker.

From our petty perspective, we boys won at the overpass. We put our victim in his place and proved how superior we were. God has called me numerous times to pray for the one we mocked, that God would work his blessing and healing. God calls both the mocker and the mocked to break the mold, and become powerful agents of healing.

Think It Through

1. How would you answer the assertion, "Mocking is a victimless crime"?

2. How does God feel about mocking and why?

3. What is mocking at its base?

4. How does a person recover from the impact of mocking? What paths of healing have been useful to you?

5. How can the person mocked become the eventual victor?

CHAPTER 15

HEALING THE STING OF REJECTION

I N THE 1950'S, when Sid was thirteen, his father sent his son from Louisiana to live with an aunt and uncle in California. He believed there were greater opportunities out west than in the racist south, where Sid, with his dark Basque complexion, was often mistaken for an African-American. Though Sid understood his dad's decision, he didn't want to leave home. Worse, his cousins did not accept him. "Why don't you go home?" they said. "We don't want you." Sid cried every day after the move.

We don't want you.

THE NEED FOR LOVE AND ACCEPTANCE

Though we may admire rugged individualists who appear not to need anyone, God has created us with a longing for love, acceptance, and relationships. It is our most basic need, and includes bonds not only with others, but with God Himself. Consider how this links with our own personality, intellect, emotions, and will.

With our minds we can know others, and with our emotions we can share what they feel—sorrow, joy, love, fear, pain, happiness, and anger. Our wills are moved by the example and motivation of others, and in turn move those around us. God has created us with the natural need to be known, to be loved, valued, affirmed, and championed.

WHAT IS REJECTION?

Rejection is words or actions conveying to a person that he or she is unwanted, unloved, or unacceptable in some way, thus of lesser value. It is a refusal to accept them. It is especially devastating to a young child when it comes from a parent or other family member. Children, at an early stage, do not have the mental ability, experience, or emotional maturity to separate the rejection from their worth as a person.

Norm Wright, counselor and author, has said, "To be rejected is to be unloved." The more significant the person is to you, the more painful is the perception of his or her rejection. Thus the rebuff of a spouse, a parent, a sibling, or a child can be one of life's most excruciating experiences.

> The rebuff of a spouse, a parent, or a child can be one of life's most excruciating experiences.

THE FACE OF REJECTION

Spurning may be done by parents who wanted no children. "You were a mistake. You shouldn't be here." "I wish you had never been born." "You should have been a boy." John was told by his mother, "We should have stopped having children before we had you."

Rejection is also demonstrated by withdrawing affection. In Connie's childhood, her father showered love and attention on a younger, blond, blue-eyed sister that fulfilled his ideal of beauty. Connie's brown hair and brown eyes didn't interest him. In addition, she had visible burn scars from a tragic household accident. The lack of her father's affection confirmed her feeling that she was damaged goods and ugly compared to other girls.

You were a mistake. You shouldn't be here.

Abuse in all its forms, whether verbal, physical, sexual, or emotional, is one of the most severe forms of rejection. A friend remembered, "The only time I saw my dad was when he beat me." Gene continually blasted his wife and children with his anger. Verbal hostility, animosity, and rage leave vivid emotional scars.

Rejection in marriage is devastating as well. It means the withdrawal of love and communication, and can be shown in physical or emotional unfaithfulness, abandonment, abuse, separation, or divorce. To children, divorce can be interpreted as rejection and abandonment.

Many of us have experienced peer rejection. Connie, who had received the severe burn, endured the taunts of children on the playground. "Let me see your scar," they would say. She felt like a sideshow freak.

Death of a loved person, such as a parent or a spouse, or even withdrawal into mental illness, can also have the impact of rejection.

DISGUISED REJECTION

Many forms of rejection remain hidden behind a guise of love. Favoritism or over-indulgence shows the parent does not care enough to keep the child within healthy bounds. Such spoiling damages by neglecting the parameters he or she needs. Melissa, idolized by her parents, entered life with many assets, but her self-centeredness limited her sensitivity to others. It contributed to the breakup of her marriage and lost communication with her children.

The opposite of spoiling, overly stern discipline and control, or over-protection, also communicates rejection. Parents who micromanage their children refuse to accept them as individuals, and fail to honor and release him. The child may feel he can never do anything right, or ever win approval. And when they are approved, it is usually for their performance, not for who they are. Parents may intend to teach high standards and the value of hard work, but some have actually communicated rejection.

> My dad didn't say 100 words to me the whole time I was growing up.

Inadequate time spent with a child is another form of rejection. It can be a parent who is absent from home excessively, perhaps due to work, or a parent who escapes from home because of a poor marriage. It may also be a parent who votes with his personal schedule. A friend said, "As a child, my dad never came to my games." Yet another said, "My dad didn't say 100 words to me the whole time I was growing up. His last words were 'Sign here!' He had driven me to the Marines to enlist, his final act to rid himself of me."

FEELINGS OF REJECTION

Rejection produces devastating feelings of being dismissed and devalued. Compared to everyone else, you feel incredibly small.

You are unable to hold up your head, because you feel devoid of worth and full of shame.

When marginalized, a person feels cut off, isolated, and alone.

Travis was rejected as a child, and being in a crowd was an excruciating experience. In his mind, all around him were persons of value; they were laughing and talking. He had no right to be there, having no place and worth. He learned to put up a front when he had to be part of a group, but it did little to hide the void and unworthiness he felt inside.

When marginalized, a person feels cut off, isolated and alone. He is an island with no connection to the mainland of other people.

SELF REJECTION

I hated that I was a piece of garbage and I think I hated myself.

If we believe the lie that we are of lesser value, we begin rejecting ourselves. One person said, "I hated that I was a piece of garbage and I think I hated myself." We can be angry at ourselves for our flaws, and angry at God for withholding the attributes that we feel lead to happiness. Each individual desperately needs to believe in his own gifts and worth. When we reject ourselves, the encouragement, compliments, or positive input from others may be shrugged off as a lie that does not match our inward message.

Often, I observe a person with talent and opportunity hopelessly mired in depression and self-rejection. It is frustrating for family and friends who long to help him see his assets but who are unable to do so.

LONGING FOR DEATH

Loren experienced increasing rejection in the workplace. Those who mocked him made the job site a living hell. Because of his sensitive nature, he found conflict painful. A job change would involve a process of many months, and he had his wife and children to support. Finally, he reached a point where dying seemed preferable to living. As a believer, however, he knew suicide was not an option. But for many people, like Greg who I talked about in chapter one, excruciating emotional pain leads them to take their own lives.

> Oh, if I could only stop living, and end the pain.

APPROVAL ADDICT

Many of us who have dealt with rejection enter a hopeless lifestyle, trying to gather enough approval to go on. Nearly every word or action is an attempt to garner enough reinforcement to make life worth living. We ignore God's view of us, and instead look to others to affirm us. If they don't, we're devastated. This response compounds our problem because when other people sense our great need, they are repelled.

> Those who most needed the Savior . . . sent Him to a humiliating death.

If you're an approval addict, consider asking yourself this question when you communicate: "Am I focused on myself, seeking validation, or am I genuinely seeking to benefit the other person?"

CHRIST WAS REJECTED

The most significant rejection in history was the spurning of the Messiah, culminating in His crucifixion.

> He came to that which was his own, but his own did not receive him.
>
> —John 1:11 N

He came to heal and save. But those He came for heaped abuse on Him and sent Him to a humiliating death.

> He was despised and rejected by men, a man of sorrows, and familiar with suffering. Like one from whom men hide their faces he was despised, and we esteemed him not.
>
> —Isaiah 53:3

THE MEASURE OF GOD'S ACCEPTANCE

The most potent antidote for rejection is acceptance by God. When we come to faith in Him, we are embraced by the Lord God Himself.

> To the praise of the glory of his grace, wherein he hath made us accepted in the beloved.
>
> —Ephesians 1:6 (KJV)

Consider some of the examples in Scripture of how greatly God loves and accepts us.

- *Not even a sparrow is forgotten before God.* He not only knows every intimate detail about you, but treasures you more than you can know. His thoughts are always toward you. (Luke 12:6-7)
- *His thoughts of you encompass intimate knowledge and deep concern.* He was present forming you in your mother's womb, orders your days, and is present in times of darkness. His caring thoughts toward you are more than you can comprehend. (Psalm 139:17-18)
- *He understands your sorrows just as if He had stored all your tears in a bottle.* He knows and bears your pain as if it were carefully inscribed in a book. He misses none of it. (Psalm 56:8)
- *He cares greatly for your welfare, and offers you hope and a future.* Though the verse is spoken of Israel, it is a picture of God's thoughts and plans for you. (Jeremiah 29:11)

> You are a treasure of infinite worth.

- *His concern for you is immediate, as if you were His nursing child, and He the mother.* He will never forget you. Though spoken of Israel, you are so close to Him it is as if you were inscribed on His hands. (Isaiah 49:15-16)

This is the verdict on your value. You are accepted because you are a treasure of infinite worth. Soak in it, meditate on it, and live every moment on the basis of it.

One of the most effective missionaries I know falls to sleep each night humming, "Jesus loves me, this I know . . . "

Evaluating Rejection

How do we counteract the crushing experiences of rejection?

- Realize that often those who reject us do so because they were rejected themselves, and are left with a great void in their own lives. They are following the pattern they experienced, and wrong others out of their own pain and emptiness.
- Decide that being minimized by others does not determine your worth. Create a new vision of yourself and your God-given gifts and how much the Lord loves you. Meditate on Scripture verses that affirm those truths.
- Take the sensitivity you experience and use it to accept others. Become their champion. Discover the greatest power in the world—the power of a friend to encourage for great good. Because you have seen the power of acceptance, use it to spur others to greatness.

I mentioned Sid at the beginning of the chapter. He found healing and wholeness in his relationship with God, and out of his own interrupted childhood, began to give to others. In 1995, he started a small, after-school basketball league to encourage children in their abilities and to impart God's great principles for living. The league grew and now regularly has over 500 students. Perhaps 6,000 children over the years have benefited from his selfless investment. Sid emerged from his childhood experience of rejection to discover he was accepted by God. Out of his own pain, Sid chose to bring love, nurture, and acceptance to others.

> Being minimized by others does not determine your worth.

Think It Through

1. Why does rejection cause such distress?

2. Why might rejection by others cause us to reject ourselves?

3. Evaluate the nature and depth of the rejection Christ experienced.

4. Why is grasping our acceptance by God so crucial in overcoming rejection?

5. Why are those who have experienced rejection powerfully equipped to help heal others?

EXPERIENCES THAT HAMPER US

CHAPTER 16

CONVERTING FAILURE TO TRUE SUCCESS

A T THE END of six years of pastoring a small church, my
agonized cry to my wife was, "I have failed!"

We entered Emmanuel, our first church after seminary, with all the dreams of youth. We would be here for the rest of our lives. It would be one glorious stream of loving people, reaching the lost, and faithfully proclaiming and teaching God's Word.

But over the six years, leadership struggles mushroomed. Strong leaders sparred over values and methods. Some sought to control all of the decisions. The tide of criticism of my ministry grew. Finally, two out of three

> I have failed. I am a failure. I will always be a failure.

of my board members felt I should resign. A vote of confidence revealed that 1/3 of the congregation did not support my ministry as their pastor.

I was well aware that I had made mistakes. In my first leadership position I showed immaturity. My pride robbed me of compassion for the brokenhearted. I based some decisions on the imperative of building my own kingdom. The tremendous price of ministry surprised me, and long hours with often little encouragement.

I concluded I had failed. My statement to Beverly meant, "I have failed myself, my family, my church, and my God!" And my conclusions edged over into the more dangerous categories of "I am a failure. I will always be a failure."

Proof of Failure?

As I arrayed the proofs in my own mind, the evidence was broader than just church conflict, though that was the major element. I considered myself a failure because my gifts did not measure up to the other prominent pastors I knew. I had a smaller church, far from the great programs or impressive numbers of which others could boast. When pastors met, they invariably compared their successes, and I felt my work came out on the short end.

I felt I had failed when people left the church, or disagreed with the content or style of my messages. Some left because we did not have a bigger youth program. Others criticized my ministry because it did not mirror the ministry of a prominent pastor heard in the media. I felt demeaned by their comparison.

But the bigger fault was mine. I had fallen prey to the idolatry of success. Consider a couple of pieces of evidence of the mindset of our day.

The Idolatry of Success

Andrew Carnegie in *The Road to Business Success* said, "I would not give a fig for the young man who does not already see himself the partner or the head of an important firm . . . Say to yourself 'My place is at the top.' Be king in your dreams."

Vince Lombardi, former coach of the Green Bay Packers said "Winning isn't everything. It's the only thing."

Failure is obvious in the sports world that idolizes success. Golfer John Daly, described as ". . . big talking, big hitting . . ." on Sunday, October 9, 2005, missed two putts at the WGC American Express Championship. The purse was worth 1.3 million dollars, in the upper hundreds of thousands better than second place. His first miss sent the tournament into sudden death. The second putt, a seeming routine one of twenty inches, handed the victory to Tiger Woods.

Tiger Woods in the same year missed one putt for $950,000 in the Skins Game, giving the win to another man.

But surely believers are immune from this humbling experience. In a reality check, Howard Hendricks has said to believers:

> Failure is one of the uglies of life. We deny it, run away from it, or, upon being overtaken, fall into permanent paralyzing fear. Probably because of our reluctance to face it, not much is written about the anatomy of failure. As Christians we wave our visionary banners proclaiming, "Victory in Christ," refusing often to admit that the path to ultimate victory may include intermediate bloody noses.
>
> —*Failure, the Back Door to Success,* Lutzer

Two Types of Failure

At the outset, it is helpful to discern two types of failure. The first is spiritual failure; the second is failure in the endeavors of life. By the first I mean sin, rebellion against God. I have dealt with sin and guilt in chapter seven, and great personal weakness in chapter eight. We have all sinned. The solution for sin is to turn to Christ the Savior, in faith, believing on Him. When believers in Christ sin, we are exhorted to repent, to turn around, confess our sin, and again order our personal life in faith and obedience, following the commands God has given in His Word.

Though we may hesitate to admit it, failure is an almost constant reality for all of us. We fail to achieve our own standards, we fall short of the goals others expect of us, and we fail to measure up to God's call to fulfill the work He has given to each of us. Beyond its experience for all of us, how do we explain its presence in the life of believers?

THE GREATEST FAILURE

What was the greatest failure of all time? Let me offer the cross of Christ. Before you reject my thought, consider the immensity of the task Christ attempted, that the objects of His Messianic ministry were not just Jews, but the whole world, every person, and every nation.

> Listen to me, you islands; hear this, you distant nations: Before I was born the LORD called me; from my birth he has made mention of my name.
>
> —Isaiah 49:1

At His appearance, and that of His forerunner, John the Baptist, the cities emptied to hear Him. He was the greatest public phenomena of His time. But despite the huge crowds, He was rejected as Lord and Messiah by the Jewish nation and its leaders:

> He came to that which was his own, but his own did not receive him.
>
> —John 1:11

After three years of public ministry, He was rejected by a crowd who said, "Crucify him!" He was rejected by the religious leaders who put Him to death through the procurator Pilate. But surely

He had an immense cloud of disciples that remained loyal. Listen to His words to His own twelve disciples:

> Then Jesus told them, 'This very night you will all fall away on account of me, for it is written: "I will strike the shepherd, and the sheep of the flock will be scattered."'
> —Matthew 26:31 (see Zechariah 13:7)

After He was captured in the Garden of Gethsemane, Scripture records: "Then all the disciples deserted him and fled" (Matthew 26:55-56).

What must have been His feelings at this point? They are reflected in Isaiah 49: "But I said 'I have labored to no purpose; I have spent my strength in vain and for nothing'" (Isaiah 49:4a).

Even though the Savior knew He had fulfilled the Father's will, do not miss the crushing human feelings of failure. From the external perspective of His mission, the wheels have fallen off.

A Fellow Failure?

In part, it is because of the defeat of His earthly mission, and the temptations and sorrows of His earthly life that He can sympathize with your feelings of failure.

> Therefore, He had to be made like His brethren in all things, so that He might become a merciful and faithful high priest in things pertaining to God, to make propitiation for the sins of the people. For since He Himself was tempted in that which He has suffered, He is able to come to the aid of those who are tempted.
> —Hebrews 2:17-18 (NASB)

He knows the frustration of laboring in vain, of being rejected by the very ones He sought to save. He saw the collapse of an immense endeavor. He was rejected more brutally than anything you have ever experienced. But of course this is only half the story. The last half of Isaiah 49:4 records the One He turned to in His seeming failure: "Yet what is due me is in the LORD's hand, and my reward is with my God" (Isaiah 49:4b).

To whom He turned in His sense of failure is important. It instructs us to whom we should turn. At the end of what He could do in His earthly life, He offers the entirety of His ministry to His Father as an offering. He leaves the outcome of His work to the court of heaven.

From a human standpoint the cross looks like a failure. But it is God's greatest success story! The Savior did not stop His work at this seeming failure, but pressed through in obedience to purchase salvation and forgiveness for all.

INSIGHTS ON FAILURE

Using the model of the Savior, and wisdom from the Scriptures, let me offer some wisdom concerning the human experience of failure.

- *Failure that is sin needs to be confessed.* Failure can possibly be God's reproof, and we need to hear God's voice of correction. When viewing failure apart from sin, I encourage you to reject blaming yourself or others. Move on to the next part of God's plan.
- *Beware of flawed yardsticks of success.* When you consider yourself a failure, what are you using as your measuring stick? Someone once said there is success that is true failure, and failure that is true success. Choose to reject human comparison that measures by a flawed, shifting standard.
- *Feelings of failure cannot be trusted.* Our feelings, though part of our God-given emotional nature, cannot be our sole guide. Feelings have been compared to a roller coaster—up

one minute, down the next. We need God's voice and wisdom.

- *Reject blaming yourself.* It will only complicate using the experience as a foundation for God's next step in your life and ministry. Take inventory as a servant under God's high call, and in your loss live out His character to others.

- *Failure is a part of the human experience.* We are all failures at something. Failure can remind us to center our life and ministry in God, and for His glory. Accept that you are frail in many areas. In your humanity, cast yourself again on God and His plan.

- *Instead of being defensive, develop a healthy sense of humor about your frailties.* This does not excuse lowering your standards, but accepting that God created us with limitations. It is part of His perfect plan.

- *Get up and move on.* Learn from failure. In chapter one, we viewed Elijah's feelings of failure. At Mt. Sinai God re-commissioned him to continue his ministry. Instead of seeing him as disqualified, God saw him as better equipped than ever.

- *Recognize that sometimes failure is part of God's plan.* God called Isaiah and Jeremiah to tasks at which they would fail from a human perspective (Isaiah 6:8-12; Jeremiah 1:17-19); they were to proclaim truth to a rebellious people. We should not settle for failure if we can succeed, but accept that, though obedient to God, we will fail at some things.

What Is True Success?

I would like to offer some of my conclusions on the nature of true success:

- *True success is knowing God and pleasing Him.* Grow in your knowledge of Him, and you will grow in your knowledge of His purpose. Paul shares his goal with us: . . . . "we are not trying to please men, but God." (1 Thess. 2:4b) This is what we have been created for. People long for romance. This is the greatest romance: growing close to our God; growing deeper in love with Him.
- *Christlike love for others is a supreme priority.* Christ stated it as a command:

> True success is knowing God and pleasing Him.

A new command I give you: Love one another. As I have loved you, so you must love one another. By this all men will know that you are my disciples, if you love one another.
—John 13:34-35

Some elements of a fuller definition of love are seeing others as of high value, a resulting concern for them, and actions to benefit them.

- *Selfless service of others.* This is the outward working of love. The Son of God set Himself as the first servant and the model for our service: "For even the Son of Man did not come to be served, but to serve . . ." (Mark 10:45 NIV). When the disciples vied for prominence Christ said, "Whoever wants to be first must be your slave" (Matthew 20:27 NIV).
- *In fulfilling God's call, you complete the work God gives you to do.* God assigns unique tasks to each of us to do. It is in completing this work that we find our highest sense of fulfillment and joy, and the greatest sense of the Savior's,

"Well done!" But work seen as complete in God's sight may look like a failure or incomplete in man's sight. An example is Christ's own declaration, "It is finished!" in John 19:30.

THE SAVIOR'S, "WELL DONE"

As I shared with Beverly my feelings that I had failed, she wisely and strongly answered "You have not failed. You have laid down your life for these sheep. God will use your investment for His glory."

Years have proven the wisdom of her words. Twenty-two years after we left, we returned to help dedicate a new facility at the church where I had cried out to God about my failure. By God's grace He blessed what we invested, and the congregation has grown to four or five times its original size. The warm hugs, tears, and sincere thank you's seemed to express the voice of God: You did not fail. Every seed you invested for My glory, I have used as I pleased. Yes, you made some mistakes, and you were learning, but I used you to do something great. Well done, good and faithful servant.

Think It Through

1. When have you most significantly experienced feelings of failure?

2. How do you see success idolized in our culture? What kinds of success are most celebrated?

3. Though we may fail in some earthly tasks, how can we begin to experience the greatest realm of success in God?

4. What may be some of God's purposes in allowing failure in our lives?

5. What sort of success will win the Savior's, "Well done!"?

CHAPTER 17

TURNING HUMILIATION INTO HEROISM

STEVE'S STEPFATHER LIKED to say, "My way or the highway!" He had become a father to three boys, ages nine, six, and four, after marrying their mother. Due to alcohol and abuse experienced from his own father, the man ruled with a heavy hand. Steve and his brothers were required to do all the chores around the house, and when he was displeased, he made them move big rocks from one part of the yard and back again. To save money at the barber, he cut the boys' hair himself. They looked like he had placed a bowl on their heads. At a time when long hair was the style, they returned to school humiliated.

> The worst was when he hit me, usually with his open hand. When he was angry, he used his fist.

Steve says, "The worst was when he hit me, usually with his open hand. When he was angry he used his fist." Often it was for small things. As a result, Steve withdrew into a shell and often withdrew to a local creek—his favorite place to be alone. "I felt terrible about myself," he says.

Have you experienced the smallness of humiliation? It could be shame from work associates who mocked or talked down to you, or the impact of multiple episodes of abuse. It could be the exposure of your own failure such as significant moral compromise or crime. Whatever the source, humiliation devastates our sense of significance.

THE SWITCH

Like Steve, the humiliations of life often galled me. I felt low, powerlessness, small, and degraded. None of us would choose such lowly feelings, and when we experience them it's easy to miss seeing them as launching pads for greatness. I was slow to understand that when I was humiliated, I was in a strategic place, close to the most powerful position a human being can possess.

> The most powerful place we can have is humility before God.

Perhaps fifteen years ago I began to grasp Bible passages that talked about the place of humility in our lives. I began to see my feelings of humiliation as a beginning point to humble myself before God, and cling closely to Him. This submission to Him, perhaps at the lowest points in life, ushers us into the realm of the greatest power we can know. Feelings of lowliness and degradation are strategic opportunities to find power with God, influence with men, and authority over our own sinful nature.

HUMILITY—A PLACE OF POWER

Why would I say that humility is a place of power, when the world says it is a place of ultimate powerlessness only for losers? Consider what the Lord says about those who have influence with Him:

> For this is what the high and lofty One says—he who lives forever, whose name is holy: "I live in a high and holy place, but also with him who is contrite and lowly in spirit, to revive the spirit of the lowly and to revive the heart of the contrite.
>
> —Isaiah 57:15

When the Lord says He chooses the contrite and lowly to dwell with Him, He is defining the kind of person with whom He desires intimate communion, and who pleases Him. The person who takes this low place of brokenness, confession, and yieldedness, can enjoy not only fellowship with Him, but a place of great influence with God.

". . . whoever humbles himself like this child is the greatest in the kingdom of heaven" (Matthew 18:4).

The disciples asked Jesus who was the greatest in the kingdom of heaven. He had a child stand among them, then said: ". . . whoever humbles himself like this child is the greatest in the kingdom of heaven" (Matthew 18:1-4).

Not only is the meek one pronounced the greatest before God, but God blesses and exalts him:

The greatest among you will be your servant. For whoever exalts himself will be humbled, and whoever humbles himself will be exalted.

—Matthew 23:11-12

OF WHAT USE IS THIS PLACE OF INFLUENCE?

A great benefit of this high place of influence is that God hears the prayer of the humble and works speedily and powerfully to answer their request: ". . . He forgetteth not the cry of the humble" (Psalm 9:12b KJV).

In Chapter Four I mentioned Luke18:1-8, the story of the widow and the dishonest judge, from the aspect of never despairing. Another aspect of the story is the small and powerless position of the widow, and her persistence before the judge. Jesus exhorts us, though we may be small in human influence, to ask boldly and persistently of God in prayer. The one who calls tirelessly in prayer, in that way, will be answered quickly.

JACOB, A MAN WITH CLAY FEET

Jacob is an example of one who transformed humiliation to humility, which is power and influence with God. As sometimes happens, Jacob's name also expressed truths about his character. Born a twin, he emerged from the womb in an unusual way: ". . . After this, his brother came out, with his hand grasping Esau's heel; so he was named Jacob" (Genesis 25:26a).

In his name and character, Jacob was a heel grabber, a supplanter. Later, when he deceived his father and cheated his brother of the blessing of the firstborn (Genesis 27:5-29), he was shown to be one who displaces others so he can have the greater place. In our world it may be the one with an inflated ego who climbs the corporate ladder, pulling others down so he or she can move up.

Jacob, a Man Seeking God

Though Jacob was human in his failings, he believed deeply in the reality of God and His blessing, which the patriarchs passed on to their sons. He was willing to risk everything to receive that blessing from his father.

In his encounter with God at Bethel (Genesis 28:10-22) he showed he wanted to do God's will. God promised to go with him wherever he went, to bless him, and to return him to Canaan. Jacob vowed that if the Lord went with him in that way, he would forever serve the Lord only as his God.

Humbled? By God?

Jacob traveled to serve his uncle Laban (Genesis 29:1-31:16), whom he found to be a greater supplanter and trickster than he was. Though seemingly taken into Laban's house as a son, Jacob was cheated in countless ways. Why would God humble Jacob, or any of us for that matter? Because we need to see our failures and make a new beginning. Is that cruel of God? It is the kindest thing He could do. Some of His most caring actions toward those He loves is to reprove them as sons. Consider what the Lord said about humbling the Jewish people during their wanderings:

> Remember how the LORD your God led you all the way in the desert these forty years, to humble you and to test you in order to know what was in your heart, whether or not you would keep his commands. He humbled you, causing you to hunger and then feeding you with manna . . . .
> —Deuteronomy 8:2-3a

Facing the Threat

The hostility from Laban and his sons grew, and God called Jacob to return to Canaan (Genesis 31:3). But his return meant a difficult challenge, facing his brother, Esau, whose intention toward him was clear:

> Esau held a grudge against Jacob because of the blessing his father had given him. He said to himself, "The days of mourning for my father are near; then I will kill my brother Jacob."
>
> —Genesis 27:41

Fearing for his life, Jacob sent a gracious message to Esau, and took a humbled posture. He hoped for mercy, but instead, the bomb dropped. Without any explanation, Jacob was told his brother was coming with four hundred men (Genesis 32:6). Remembering Esau's sworn purpose, there was little doubt in Jacob's mind that Esau's purpose was to kill him, his wives, children, and servants, brutally fulfilling his vow. Abject terror gripped Jacob. His earlier lying and deceit when he stole Esau's blessing caught up with him. Though Jacob's selfish actions did not justify murder, the threat to all of them could be placed at Jacob's feet.

Esau was coming to kill him.

PRAYER: DOING THE RIGHT THING

Though humiliated by his moment of crisis, Jacob did the right thing. He humbled himself before God in prayer. He pleaded with every fiber of his being for God to deliver him. It's interesting to note that the Lord had already promised rescue.

- At Bethel, where the Lord promised to watch over him, and give Canaan to him and his descendants. (Genesis 28:13-15)

- At the Lord's call to return to Canaan, He promised to be with him. (Genesis 31:3, 11-13)
- At Machanaim, a place where the angels of God met him as he journeyed. It evidenced that God's camp of angels, though unseen, were there to protect him. (Genesis 32:1-2)

Despite these repeated assurances, Jacob remained intimidated, and pleaded for protection (Genesis 32:9-12). His prayer was not just for himself but for all those with him: ". . . for I am afraid he will come and attack me, and also the mothers with their children" (Genesis 32:11b).

In his prayer and actions he becomes a rescuer of others.

THE WRESTLING MATCH

Though he had humbled himself and prayed fervently, he was still filled with dread. He placed his company over the river, then returned to spend the night by himself. There God met him, as He meets us in our darkest hour. In an unprecedented, unique encounter, the Lord chose to depict Jacob's protection and victory in a wrestling match.

> So Jacob was left alone, and a man wrestled with him till daybreak.
> —Genesis 32:24

The strangest thing about the struggle was that the Lord allowed Himself to be beaten in order to illustrate to Jacob that he was victorious in his urgent request. In the declaration of his victory the Lord states, ". . . you have struggled with God and with men and have overcome" (Genesis 32:28b), Not only does the Lord highlight Jacob's victory, but He renames Jacob from *supplanter* to a name that means *one who fights with God and prevails:* "Then the man said, "Your name will no longer be Jacob, but Israel" (Genesis 32:28a).

A SUNRISE AND A LIMP

The wrestling match and name change had immense significance. Not only was Jacob given a vivid picture of the answer to his urgent request but his very identity and character were transformed by God.

> The Lord allowed Himself to be beaten in order to illustrate to Jacob that he had been victorious in his urgent request.

Because the event changed everything, he was given an injury to remember its significance; he walked away with a limp. God had met Jacob and changed his character. He also walked into a sunrise (Genesis 32:31), a picture of his new beginning.

POWER WITH GOD AND MEN

Like Jacob, God desires that instead of surrendering to the shame of humiliation, we choose to humble ourselves before Him, the place of true influence and greatness. Just as it was for Jacob (Gen. 32:28), this place is . . .

- *A place of power with God.* It is the humble person who has fellowship with Him, and whose cry and prayer He answers in power.
- *A place of power with men.* God softened his brother's heart. When Esau met him, instead taking violent action, he fell on his neck and kissed him (Genesis 33:4). God moves people in answer to prayer.

- *A place of authority over ourselves.* Brokenness and humility bring us to our right place under God's rule. Humiliation in life can bring us afresh to accept God's discipline, and walk carefully, knowing our feet are made of clay.

THE END OF THE STORY

Though Steve and his brothers were humiliated by the severe discipline of their stepfather, they endured because of their love for their mother. At one point, Doug, the youngest boy, ran away and did not return home for a few weeks. When he came back, he was noticeably different. He had come in contact with a Christian family who led him to faith in Christ. Steve saw in his brother the peace and assurance he longed for. He too knelt and decided for Christ.

This decision initiated a new sunrise in his life. Steve pursued training in construction, became involved in nation-wide projects, then began his own business as a licensed contractor. He later met Jody, who came from a Christian family, and he began to learn the love that Christ can bring to a home. They married, had three children, and Steve's loving fathering became a model to those around him. He became a leader in Scouting, and he was led to use his construction experience as Director of Buildings and Grounds for a large church where he continues to influence thousands.

Instead of allowing his childhood humiliation to scar his life, Steve chose Christ, a new identity, and a life as God's humble servant. He continues to live as a man of power and influence under God, helping to change the world for good.

Think It Through

1. In what situations have you experienced humiliation?

2. What does the author mean by *choosing to humble ourselves*? How can humiliation lead us to humility? How does humility differ from human feelings of powerlessness and degradation?

3. What is the value of humility before God? Why would the author say it is a place of power?

4. Why did God appear before Jacob as a wrestler? In the wrestling match, what was He revealing to Jacob?

5. How can true humility be a place of power?

CHAPTER 18

MOVING FROM ISOLATION TO FRIENDSHIP

I ARRIVED HOME from work anticipating the healing presence of my wife and my children. It was the best time of the day. I flopped on the overstuffed den chair as David, twelve, our Little League catcher; Chandra, nine, our carrot-topped singer, April, seven, everybody's friend, and Joelle, five, our pet lover greeted me and continued their evening activities.

My day had started in a rush with a 6:00 a.m. breakfast meeting, then an urgent call from a friend. My mother had fallen again. In addition to visiting her, the day included a staff meeting, a stack of telephone contacts, and planning for upcoming events. Despite all my high-stress activities and constant contact with people, I ministered in a relationship vacuum apart from my family.

> You don't have any male friends.

Can a confirmed loner ever open up to friendship?

I clicked the evening news off and turned to my wife, Beverly. "How was your day?"

As a sixteen-year veteran of my stressful, low relationship lifestyle, she looked deeply into my eyes and said, "Do you realize you don't have any male friends?"

"Yes, I do," I said, defending myself. "I have lots of friends. Everybody's my friend." As if my statement were the last word, I walked out of the room. Neither of us opened the topic again that evening. Wisely, Bev left me to ponder my fantasy.

Because of hurts in childhood, including conflict between my parents, I emerged from childhood with the belief that *You never know who will stick you.* I avoided close relationships and hid behind a barrier of my own making. I pretended to be self-sufficient; I didn't need anyone. But inwardly, feelings of smallness and inadequacy dominated me.

MORE COMFORTABLE WITH THINGS THAN PEOPLE

Through college I was a loner walking around in my dad's worn WWII army jacket. Afterwards, in military service, I was more comfortable with airplanes than people. As a transport (Air Force C-7A in Vietnam) and hospital ship (C-118) pilot and aircraft commander, I felt at home in the sky. It is still true today.

> Why do I need anybody? Can't I take care of myself?

When I'm facing what appear to be unsolvable people problems, I love to climb in an airplane, a definitive world governed by invariable principles. The blue California sky, fleecy clouds, and rural landscape wash over my soul in a healing wave.

The night after my wife's statement, grasping for sleep, I debated with God.

"I'm a real man," I protested. "I don't need blubbering relationships where we cry on each other's shoulders. Why do I need anybody? Can't I take care of myself?" Then I used the excuse to which many leaders resort: "How can you lead if people know your weaknesses?"

Though I rationalized that I was a friend to all, increasingly I saw that I was a friend of none. I had chosen the curse of isolation. Yet deep within, I longed for the close relationships I had rejected because of fear.

Issues of self worth surfaced. "Am I worthy of an eyeball-to-eyeball relationship with another person? Do I have anything to bring to the table?"

REASONS MEN ARE FRIENDLESS

In his book *The Friendless American Male*, David W. Smith, has tabbed many reasons men, particularly, tend to be friendless:

- They are taught to suppress their emotions. "Big boys don't cry."
- They find it hard to admit a need for friendship. Relationships often remain on a superficial level.
- They idolize strong, independent, self-sufficient role models.
- They are often overly competitive, and may view others as a threat to winning.
- They are often reluctant to ask for help. "Stand on your own two feet!"
- They are raised to believe that success is more important than relationship.

"And Jonathan made a covenant with David because he loved him as himself" (1 Samuel 18:1b).

DAVID AND JONATHAN

Troubled by a night of unanswered questions, the next morning I reached for my Bible. "Lord, Beverly's right, but where do I go from here? The idea of emerging from my cave terrifies me. I have no idea where to start."

Seeking guidance from the Bible, I began to discover patterns of friendship interlaced throughout the Scriptures. The remarkable bond between Jonathan and David jumped off the pages. There was no lack of masculinity here.

After David's victory over Goliath, Jonathan, who had seen David minister to Saul, his troubled father, committed to a stronger bond between them.

> After David had finished talking with Saul, Jonathan became one in spirit with David, and he loved him as himself. From that day Saul kept David with him and did not let him return to his father's house. And Jonathan made a covenant with David because he loved him as himself. Jonathan took off the robe he was wearing and gave it to David, along with his tunic, and even his sword, his bow and his belt.
>
> —1 Samuel 18:1-4

The bond these two developed would last until Jonathan was killed in battle. They stood by each other through dark days, when Saul sought to take David's life. The mutual tenderness between strong warriors amazed me. Their giving and receiving was genuine, and neither was threatened. David and Jonathan modeled the closeness that friendship can provide. They illustrate peer friendship, a first level of relationship.

CHRIST AND THE TWELVE

When Christ came to earth, He chose to enter into close relationship with those who loved Him. Addressing His disciples, He says, "I have called you friends" (John 15:15b). Here is Jesus—who is God in the flesh—calling ordinary, finite men, His friends. We might assume that when He entered the realm of earth He would maintain a separateness. But though He perfectly maintained the holiness of God, Jesus entered into a relationship with the twelve and others. Jesus tells us He is always willing to enter into relationship with those who love Him. His call to the twelve was one beginning point in initiating earthly friendships.

> Jesus went up on a mountainside and called to him those he wanted, and they came to him. He appointed twelve—designating them apostles—that they might be with him and that he might send them out to preach.
>
> —Mark 3:13-14

Notice that His first assignment was not a call to work, but to be with Him. In his classic *The Master Plan of Evangelism,* Robert E. Coleman says, "Amazing as it may seem, all Jesus did to teach these men His way was to draw them close to Himself. He was His own school and curriculum."

Let's consider three levels of friendship, two of them modeled by Christ. The first is peer friendship. Jesus bonded with the twelve at this level. However, He developed a deeper relationship with three of His disciples. Proof of their closeness is seen when He took these three to the mountain where He was transfigured, and revealed more of His glory (Matthew 17:1-3). It also seems that His closest peer relationship was with John.

The Savior's bond with the twelve also demonstrated a second level of friendship—mentoring others. In mentoring, one person disciples another who desires to grow in some area of development. The Savior's mentoring through His investment of love and nurture would transform these into men who would then turn the world upside down.

PAUL AND TIMOTHY

A third level of friendship is demonstrated by one receiving mentoring. This is seen in Timothy's strong bond with the apostle Paul. Timothy submitted to Paul's mentoring:

> Paul came also to Derbe and to Lystra. And a disciple was there, named Timothy, the son of a Jewish woman who was a believer, but his father was a Greek, and he was well spoken of by the brethren who were in Lystra and Iconium. Paul wanted this man to go with him . . .
>
> —Acts 16:1-3a

Timothy was the one being built up by one more mature. He learned his lessons well, as reflected in Paul's letter to Philippi.

> I hope in the Lord Jesus to send Timothy to you soon, that I also may be cheered when I receive news about you. I have no one else like him, who takes a genuine interest in your welfare. For everyone looks out for his own interests, not those of Jesus Christ. But you know that Timothy has proved himself, because as a son with his father he has served with me in the work of the gospel.
>
> —Philippians 2:19-22

We need all three levels of friendship: peer relationship, mentoring others, and being mentored by someone more mature.

Natural Loners?

Aren't some men and women called to be loners, or are they by nature more disposed to live apart from relationship? What about Elijah in his prophetic ministry? If there ever was a born loner, Elijah seems to be one. His isolated stand for God in an idolatrous nation led him to live in a cave. He had limited human encouragement. But in his despair on Mt. Sinai, even Elijah was told to link up with another human being.

> The LORD said to him, "Go back the way you came, and go to the Desert of Damascus. When you get there, anoint . . . Elisha son of Shaphat from Abel Meholah to succeed you as prophet.
> —1 Kings 19:15-16

The Lord directed him to develop a relationship with Elisha, who would succeed him as prophet. This was critical following his despair over the confrontation at Mt. Carmel. After the anointing, the Bible says of his protégé, Elisha, "Then he set out to follow Elijah and became his attendant" (1 Kings 19:21b). Elijah had been faithful during his days alone, but now God addressed his need for companionship. God has designed us for friendship as well, no matter how much of a loner we might think we are.

The Next Step

After I saw the pattern of friendship in Scripture, the Lord seemed to say, "You have enough information; now get started. Begin with one."

How does a person initiate friendship? Proverbs says that one who wants to have friends "must show himself friendly" (Proverbs 18:24b AV).

I needed a secure place to begin and Sid's Gym in a local mall offered that possibility. Often Jack Freeberg worked out with me.

He was a muscular senior in his mid-sixties, of medium height and graying hair. I respected Jack, a man of faith, ex-military, even as I was, and a community leader. I could see from his genuine smile and easygoing manner that he was open to friendship.

As I walked toward the mall, gym bag in hand, the blossoming of spring foliage contrasted to the deadness in my soul. Fear gripped me as I approached the front entrance.

"Can I really open this door in my life? What will it mean? How will my life change?" I walked out onto the gym floor with its scent of sweat and baby oil. Full-length mirrors reflected rows of barbells. The squeak of Universal machines combined with the thump of workout music. Then I saw him.

"Hi Jack. How's it going?"

"Hey Jonnie. Good to see you. How are you doing today?" His warm response was like a balm.

"Pretty good, except I'm concerned about my mother; she has lymphoma cancer and is falling a lot."

From this unpretentious beginning, our friendship grew. During our workouts two or three times a week, we shared joys and concerns as we pumped weights. In coming months the topics spanned the death of my mom, Jack's heart surgery, then a few years later, the death of his wife. Over the next few years, because of closures, our workouts moved to other gyms, and now we more often meet at a local donut shop.

In the beginning moments of our friendship, there were no tears or nonstop gushes. Without verbalizing it, I quietly let down the barriers, received him, and offered myself. Slowly, I realized that he had long before received me. It took a few days to evaluate what was happening. All I knew was:

"Wow! I'm still alive!" This was a whole new world to me.

"Wait a minute. This is fun." I began anticipating our times together. Just driving to the gym I could feel the tension draining away.

Like a successful chemist, I considered expanding the scale of my experiment. A Tuesday Bible study offered a second opportunity to be with warm-hearted men I respected. This time I was not entering blind. I had the experience of one budding friendship, and was beginning to get a feel for selfless interchange and acceptance.

I picked a Tuesday, and opened a second door. The reception of these men, starting with a few, was just as open and inviting as the pancakes, bacon, and coffee that began our meeting. The morning group spawned a golf group on Fridays.

The growing adventure of friendship flooded my life with encouragement. When I opened up and offered myself, others usually, though not always, met me with an equal offer. It was a foundation of well-being and support similar to my relationship with the Lord, with my wife Beverly, and my great kids. As I extended friendship to others, I discovered the life-changing power of love, and others began to blossom and grow. I discovered the great influence of a friend in changing lives for good, even as I had been changed.

In some ways the most powerful person in the world is a friend, someone who believes in you. The sign over my life once read "PRIVATE: No Admittance." But the Lord, my Divine Friend, has raised the curtains on the windows of my private life, and flipped over the sign to read "OPEN: Welcome!"

Can a confirmed loner open up to friendship? Yes, by opening doors with God's help.

Think It Through

1. Have you ever lived in a relationship vacuum? Why did it happen?

2. What are the most significant risks or costs for you in building relationships?

3. What were the mutual benefits for Paul and Timothy in their partnership?

4. Are some people just naturally loners? Should they remain that way?

5. What is the life-changing power of friendship?

CHAPTER 19

CONQUERING WORRY WITH TRUST

I BATTLED STOP-AND-GO traffic on the freeway when the frantic call came from Chandra, my twenty-eight-year-old daughter. I could hear her voice breaking. "Dad, Tim and I have been in a bad car accident. We're in Nebraska and we slid on black ice and hit a truck. A pipe carried by the truck came through the windshield and just missed me. Tim is bleeding, but I think I'm okay. Just pray I won't lose the baby."

> Just pray for my baby. I don't want to lose the baby.

As Bev and I raised our four children, our family had been relatively free from emergencies. Tim and Chandra were in full-time Christian work, and had joyfully announced Chandra's pregnancy two months before the accident.

Fighting tears, my own voice breaking, I hurriedly mobilized other family members for prayer, and put Chandra in touch with a registered nurse.

Then came the test.

Would I trust God, or would I worry?

As I wrestled with our crisis, I was drawn magnetically to a passage I had considered too simplistic, the one about birds and lilies in the Sermon on the Mount:

> Therefore I tell you, do not worry about your life, what you will eat or drink; or about your body, what you will wear. Is not life more important than food, and the body more important than clothes?
>
> —Matthew 6:25

As I meditated on this passage, God's instructions flooded me with peace.

Worry, a Way of Life

Worry seems a routine part of life to many of us. We often joke about it, but the Bible says it is sin, and sin of any shade separates us from God. One joking rationalization says: "It's a good thing I worry. If I left everything to you, nothing would get accomplished!" After all, isn't worry a part of diligence? Doesn't it show that I am taking appropriate responsibility for my affairs?

> It's a good thing I worry. If I left everything to you, nothing would get accomplished!

In asking us not to worry, is God teaching empty-headedness, carelessness, or a refusal to shoulder our load? The Greek word for "worry" used in Matthew 6:25 is *merimnao*, meaning anxious care, something out of bounds of the life of trust that God commands. The Word of God carefully and repeatedly warns against rampant anxiety. It is not to be confused with the legitimate load of concern for our responsibilities.

Track with me as I highlight some of God's truths that assist in dealing with the great plague of worry or anxious care.

WORRY FORGETS GOD'S GREATER GIFT OF LIFE

The question *What is life?* flows from Matthew 6:25 as quoted above. The Lord says that it is more than the food it takes to sustain it, but how much more?

Life is a gift from God to be treasured. We are the high point of God's creative work, with a higher capacity to reflect His glory than the rest of creation. We enjoy a fleeting chance to glorify and serve in our earthly life.

After God gave man his physical body He breathed into it the breath of life. The body is called a cup or vessel intended to be filled with the Holy Spirit, yielded to the Master's purposes and use. It is also pictured as a temple (2 Timothy 2:20-22), set apart for the service and worship of God. Would He who gave us the higher gift of life, not give us the lesser gifts needed to sustain it?

> Would the Creator of this temple . . . not give what is needed to sustain it?

WORRY IGNORES GOD'S PURPOSE TO PROVIDE

Look at the birds of the air; they do not sow or reap or store away in barns, and yet your heavenly Father feeds them. Are you not much more valuable than they?

—Matthew 6:26

The birds need food, but neither sow nor reap to provide for their future, as man does. They depend day-by-day and moment-by-moment on God's faithful provision. This supply is not so small and routine that it is disconnected from His conscious purpose. By intent, God feeds them. This is true of every single sparrow, and each one of us. Would God take care of birds, but neglect His own children? It would be like a man providing for his flocks, but letting his children starve.

Would God take care of birds, but neglect His own children?

Why are we called "more valuable"? Is God dismissing His animal creation? We have been created in the image of God, with the greater gifts of mind, emotions, will, and a spiritual capacity to know God (Genesis 1:31). These gifts give us the opportunity, if we choose, to glorify or please God. If He provides abundantly for the more humble parts of His creation, how much more will He provide for us?

WORRY SUBTRACTS

Who of you by worrying can add a single hour to his life?
—Matthew 6:27

The question about adding a cubit to our height, or an hour to our life, are examples. The Savior could have said, "Who of you by worrying has created a single morsel of food . . . a single garment . . . a single dollar?"

People caught up in anxiety live in an imaginary world of their fears.

I heard of a man whose wife worried constantly. He proposed an experiment. "Honey, for a couple of months, I would like you to keep a list of everything you worry about." She kept a careful diary, then after a period of weeks, they looked at the record. Of the things that had troubled her, none had happened. Other events had occurred that they could not have foreseen, but they were not on the list. When we worry, we waste energy and accomplish nothing.

People caught up in anxiety live in an imaginary world of fears and reality is lost. It can harm mental health and deteriorate physical health. There are professional men in their twenties having heart attacks from stress.

WORRY IGNORES GOD'S BEAUTIFYING

And why do you worry about clothes? See how the lilies of the field grow. They do not labor or spin. Yet I tell you that not even Solomon in all his splendor was dressed like one of these.
—Matthew 6:28-29

Having cited the animal creation, Jesus now turns to the plant creation and the beauty of the flowers. Their pleasing appearance displays God's glory and purposed design. In comparison, He points to the dazzling appearance of the most glorious king within their frame of reference, Solomon.

No matter how big the field of our observation (e.g. the universe via the Hubble telescope) or how small (e.g. a DNA strand under an electron microscope), we see God's design and beauty displayed in the universe. Refusing the world's flawed evaluation of appearance and excessive concern, we rest in a God who has blessed and beautified us in many ways.

> Just as God displays His glory, beauty, and design in the plant creation, so He does even more for us.

Worry Refuses to Trust

If that is how God clothes the grass of the field, which is here today and tomorrow is thrown into the fire, will he not much more clothe you, O you of little faith?

—Matthew 6:30

In this verse, Jesus emphasizes the brevity of the life of a plant. Yet He sustains even this transient part of His handiwork. In contrast, we have an immortal soul, which God will sustain forever.

When we indulge unbelief, we place ourselves in a different universe than the one where God reigns. One person called it a divided mind, like putting one foot in the things of God, and one in a world where God is absent or impotent. Our lack of trust separates us from the true God, who lovingly follows us and our affairs, ministers to our needs, and guides our course in perfect wisdom. We yield instead to great insecurity and risk.

Trusting God places us in His world where we yield to His sovereignty, lordship, and care.

Worry Forgets that God Knows Our Needs

So do not worry, saying, "What shall we eat?" or "What shall we drink?" or "What shall we wear?" For the pagans run after all these things, and your heavenly Father knows that you need them.

—Matthew 6:31-32

The Lord's repeated command not to worry (also given in Matt. 6:25 above) reminds us that worry is at its worst rebellion against God, and at the very least doubting what He has promised.

God knows our real needs more intimately than we do. Our own perception is strongly influenced by our lusts and desires. These worries and concerns are the preoccupation of those who do not trust a loving God who cares. The questions about whether we will have enough food, drink, or clothing, are part of the endless uncertainties of life. They are the lot of those who do not believe that He will provide their needs.

Earthly fathers are only a faint copy of the Heavenly. God means for us to live dependent on His constant care for His children, consumed by His love, and astounded by His perfect provision.

> Worries and concerns are the preoccupation of those who do not know a loving God who cares.

WORRY REJECTS GOD AND HIS KINGDOM

But seek first his kingdom and his righteousness, and all these things will be given to you as well.

—Matthew 6:33

When we wholeheartedly seek the kingdom of God, we reject the priorities of the world around us. God exhorts us to seek Him primarily, then the principles of living He has designed for the kingdom He governs. Righteousness is the character He intends for His own, by the power of the Holy Spirit. It is the very character of our Lord, who is slowly transforming us as we grow in Him.

Worry displaces our focus from God to the temporal things that trouble us. Habitually we gaze at our problems and inwardly dramatize things that may occur. God receives only a cursory glance, if that. We must

> We must reverse our focus: gaze at God, then glance at our problems.

reverse our focus: gaze at God, then glance at our problems.

When we live in fellowship with the Father as His obedient, trusting children, He provides what we need. And as we grow in His likeness, we learn more clearly what our needs really are.

WORRY REDIRECTS NECESSARY RESOURCES

Therefore do not worry about tomorrow, for tomorrow will worry about itself. Each day has enough trouble of its own.

—Matthew 6:34

Worry always wastes mental, emotional, and spiritual resources needed for the daily challenges God gives us. In our daily warfare we have spiritual armor, fellow soldiers who fight beside us, and the powerful artillery of prayer. God has given us all we need for the conflict and we cannot waste our mental resources worrying about the future. Our assets must be used for the opportunities each day brings. As we confront them, and trust and obey God, He goes with us and provides what we need. In this process, moment by moment, we become more than conquerors through Him who loved us (Romans 8:37).

WHY WOULD GOD NOT PROVIDE?

And my God will meet all your needs according to his glorious riches in Christ Jesus.

—Philippians 4:19

There are times in our experience when it seems like the Lord has not provided what we need, and what we have asked for. I have ministered to those faced with job loss, desperate illness, or death of precious family members. In many cases it seems that God has not answered.

The Lord sometimes allows a need to exist to meet a greater need, such as drawing us closer to Himself, or teaching us more about His nature.

When God does not answer, we must understand that He *is* the answer. Seek Him.

As I followed Tim and Chandra through the next steps after the accident, the ambulance took them to a hospital where they were determined to be in good condition, despite significant bruising, cuts, and much soreness. An ultrasound determined the baby, soon to be born Claire Innes, was fine.

Long ago I had yielded Beverly and our children to God's purposes, whatever He willed for them. He could take them if He wished and I would trust His perfect plan.

Yes, God guarded me from worry and He was faithful in caring for my three loved family members. In a time of great trial, the birds and the lilies were my teachers. God is worthy of my trust, not only concerning my most precious treasures, but in all the moment-by-moment affairs of life.

Think It Through

1. In what situations are you most prone to worry?

2. In what sense does worry subtract?

3. In what way does worry reject God and His kingdom?

4. How does worry redirect your needed mental resources?

5. Why would God not provide for a need?

REBUILDING FROM SMALLNESS

CHAPTER 20

EMERGING INTO HOPE AND CONFIDENCE

M Y FRIEND DENNIS' statement shocked me: "The reason you are having trouble trusting God today is that you have forgotten what He did yesterday." Though frank words, he had earned the right to speak as we had a close relationship. I could not deny the truth of what he said. He had observed the turmoil of fear and insecurity that dominated me. As we were students, my crisis often focused on looming examinations and papers.

He proposed a test solution. "Keep a journal, a record each day of the ways you see God at work. As you face fresh challenges, look back at the way God has shown Himself."

As I began to record evidences of God, I not only saw startling answers to prayer, but also miracles that only God could have performed. The journal

> "The reason you're having trouble trusting God today is that you have forgotten what He did yesterday."

became a resource, reminding me that God was always adequate for the doubts and fears of life.

My friend showed the value of wise counsel in a caring friendship. But insightful counsel is only one of the many tools that I have found life-changing.

WHAT MADE THE DIFFERENCE?

Recently I shared an area of struggle with a friend and said things were different now that I had discovered and implemented God's answers. Puzzled, she asked questions I often hear: "What made the difference? What happened to change things?"

Following are some of the practical tools I found of great value in my search. Wise counsel from Dennis is just one example.

MENTORING

"Why don't you come down to San Jose for a couple of days and spend some time with me?"

The invitation from one of the men I most respected astounded me. Doug was a campus representative of a Christian ministry at San Jose State University. His teaching at a Bible class was revolutionizing my life and faith as a college student.

It was the first time I could recall anyone asking to spend time with me other than my parents. He thought enough of me to impart himself.

Credible, selfless mentors make a powerful impact in shaping us.

Contrary to the religious fanatic stereotype I had of all ministers and Christian workers, he seemed normal—just like me. I saw his commitment to the Gospel as we shared the message of Christ with a student in a jammed coffee shop. Wise, godly leadership was evident as he led a planning session. I saw the loving sacrifices he made for his wife, and even came to idolize the model of Volvo he drove.

The time he invested? Comparatively little. The impact? Immense.

TARGETED BOOKS

I related earlier my feelings of failure in my first church. Those emotions were not new, but a continuation of internal warfare concerning significance. Comparing myself with others was one broad base of that struggle.

One day, I noticed a book, *Failure, the Back Door to Success.* I asked myself, *What is this, a book on failure? What is it, an instruction manual?* Being the self-crowned king of failure, I could give the author some pointers. But the book dealt with recovering from failure, something common to the human experience. I grabbed the book and drank in its truths. It began with the story of a professional burdened by such a sense of failure that he took his own life.

> Targeted books can help set emotions aside and think biblically through difficult issues.

The Lord seemed to say, "Your whole definition of failure and success is desperately flawed. Look for the meaning of true success in Me instead of in comparison with others."

Targeted books can help us set emotions aside and think biblically through difficult issues.

BIBLICAL DIAGNOSIS AND CURE

Earlier I shared my chronic problem with despair. The solution began while studying the Bible with others. God can work powerfully when we join with others in grappling with His truth in the Scriptures.

As with other areas of struggle, like a doctor, the Lord diagnosed my need. Though pained, I finally yielded to the verdict of the Divine Physician. I spent months exploring my deficit as I poured over the Scriptures. I carefully searched for the extent of this disease in my nature and the damage it had done and was still doing.

> When we allow the Lord to diagnose our need . . . we are on our way to a transformed life.

As I fully acknowledged that my life had been built on lies, the Lord began to instruct me. I discovered a study of the great prophet Elijah by F. B. Meyer. I traveled with this lonely messenger through his isolation, his victory at Carmel, and his hopelessness following Queen Jezebel's threat. (I have related my conclusions about Elijah in Chapter One.) In that book and study, I found answers for my own struggle.

But how could I live in the truth I had learned? I fought the tendency to remain immobile, to sit and do nothing. I discovered again as I had in the past that healing is found in obedience. When I took the first steps to obey, the power of God strengthened me.

When we allow the Lord to diagnose our need, then step out to live a different life in His power, we are on our way to a healthy life.

PRAYER

On another occasion, a crisis in a friendship emerged and I despaired of restoring the relationship. Things would not work out this time; they could not work out. I feared the worst and in my desperation cried out to God. On this occasion His answer was not the soft parental one I had expected. He seemed to say, "Stop whining and ask Me to do something!" I needed to break the grip of self-pity and get moving. Prayer changed things. It is set apart by God as the most powerful tool He's given to His people.

I love studying about the universe, stars, galaxies, and incredibly powerful phenomena such as supernovas. The cloudy band of stars we observe on a dark night is called the Milky Way, our own galaxy 100,000 light-years wide. When you pray, whether you can see it or not, nothing is ever the same. It is as if all the stars and galaxies suddenly started spinning in different directions.

> When you pray . . . nothing is ever the same. It is as if all the stars and galaxies suddenly started spinning in different directions.

DISCOVER YOUR GIFTS

Yearly at Christmas, a friend prepared a stunning program with hundreds of people involved in choir, orchestra, staging, and media. I cried inwardly, *If only I could do something like that, I would know my life was significant and I was making a meaningful impact.*

Though it seemed small, I assisted by preparing materials for attendees who had questions about Christ, the focus of the presentation. I talked with those who responded to the program,

> If only I could do something like that, I would know my life was significant and I was making a meaningful impact.

202 · LORD, I FEEL SO SMALL!

showing them how Jesus' person and message provided the answers for life.

After a few years of assisting in this way, I gained more clarity. It was as if the Lord affirmed that He had indeed chosen to use my friend, but had on equal footing also chosen to use me. My role was no less a concert played for His glory.

God wants to use you in unique ways as well. He wants you to see your dream of giftedness and usefulness fulfilled before your eyes, and have the time of your life doing it.

SPIRITUAL GIFTS: WHAT ARE THEY?

When I was young in the faith, Bob, a Christian worker asked me, "Do you know what your spiritual gifts are?" I didn't even know what he meant. His question compelled me to search for an answer. I would not see the fuller picture for more than twenty years. In his book *Discover Your Spiritual Gift and Use It* Rick Yohn has defined them as, "Special abilities that God gives you to accomplish His work." They are individual areas of giftedness freely bestowed by God. As recipients, we owe Him praise and thanks, and are accountable for the use of these capabilities.

Do you know what your spiritual gifts are?

Do all believers in Christ receive spiritual gifts? Yes, according to Ephesians: "But to each one of us grace has been given as Christ apportioned it" (Ephesians 4:7).

Though some gifts are given to leaders who minister to all, each bestowal and each individual is equally important to God.

How we exercise our gifts is important as well. We need to use them in a selfless, humble, teachable manner, the product of the Holy Spirit's presence and work in our lives.

But the fruit of the Spirit is love, joy, peace, patience, kindness, goodness, faithfulness, gentleness and self-control. Against such things there is no law.

—Galatians 5:22-23

We are all favored recipients, and our response to the gifts of others is also important. We should not neglect our own gifts; but instead of applauding them alone we must affirm, esteem, and encourage others, and spur them on to be all that they can be.

How Do I Find My Gifts?

Although my search encompassed twenty years, your own need not be as difficult or puzzling. Here are some tools:

- Comprehensive courses on spiritual gifts will give you a survey of what the gifts are. Some resources are listed in Appendix 2. Not all agree exactly on which gifts are valid today, or the number or importance of certain gifts, but there is little disagreement about their existence and purpose.
- Insights from others as they observe you aids in determining where you excel. Ask others about where your strengths lie.
- Ask yourself, "What do I enjoy doing as I serve others? Where do I find personal fulfillment?"

> Learn by doing, even if initially you're unsure which gifts are yours.

- Where is your ministry most fruitful? Where is it productive, bringing lasting results?
- Learn by doing, even if initially you're unsure which gifts are yours.

Tips on Using Your Gifts

- *Be willing to minister strenuously with your abilities.* Don't be satisfied with doing a little. We reap the greatest satisfaction when we work hard.
- *Be selfless.* Set your purpose not on acclaim or your own agenda, but to bless and benefit others.
- *Be trained to use your gift effectively.* It will increase the measure of your resources. Be a perpetual student in your area of ministry.
- *Balance your service with all other aspects of life.* Keep work, ministry, and relaxation in proper relationship.

Can God Use Me?

When in the military, I doubted that God could ever use my miniscule abilities. I met Clay* in a poor part of Angeles City near my base in the Philippines and began to share with him some of the truths of Scripture. He had fallen victim to some of the many temptations available outside the base. As the opportunity with my friend grew, it became a test case in my own mind: *Lord, if You use me to reach this one, I will never again doubt that I or my gifts are of use to You.*

> Lord, if you use me to reach Clay, I will never again doubt that I or my gifts are of use to You.

It initiated a great contest in my life and I prayed almost constantly for Clay. At a chapel in Okinawa, I was again praying for him when an earthquake shook the chapel. It seemed the Lord was saying, "I have heard you. I will use you to bring Clay to faith."

---

*Not his real name.

After some months he registered for a servicemen's retreat, and there received Christ as His Savior. Not only had God brought this man to faith, but He had proven that He could use me. God can use you, too.

It's a Long Journey

On the plain of Marathon, about twenty-five miles from Athens, Greece, an historic battle occurred in 490 B.C., when King Darius of Persia ordered his powerful armies to conquer the country. They landed their force on the plain and the Greeks observed them for a few days. Miltiades, the Greek general, concentrated his strength on the two ends of his line, and attacked the Persians with a great running charge. The superior weapons and strength of the Greeks proved decisive as they drove the Persians to their ships. The Greeks lost 192 men, while the encircled Persians lost 6,400.

The Persian ships then headed for Athens, and there was danger that the Athenians would surrender, feeling the cause was hopeless. A runner had to carry the news of the victory at Marathon to Athens. Pheidippides was chosen, though he had just carried dispatches to Sparta, and fought all day in the battle. He accepted the job and raced twenty-five miles to Athens, gasping, "Rejoice, we conquer!" before falling dead from exertion.

For many of us, life has seemed a hopeless, exhausting struggle to discover our significance, our place under God's sun. Through sixty years of life, my own spirit seemed to cry, *Lord I feel so small!* I had much in common with my friend, Greg, who took his own life. He thought he was nothing. Sadly, he missed his own greatness.

In sharing my own journey, I have focused on the satisfying answers found in God, the Bible, and in His provision for all humanity. God calls you to a new, heroic, and courageous adventure in living.

Like the run of Pheidippedes, the journey is long and demanding. In my own life, each breakthrough has been revolutionary and the springboard for a whole new way of life. Thank you for joining me in exposing the lies that demean us and discovering instead the miracle of God's purpose. My prayer for you is that you would join me in walking into a new sunrise of hope, fulfillment, and joy, and be equipped for a life of unshakeable confidence in God. Together let our lives shout, *Rejoice, we conquer!* For God's glory.

Think It Through

1. What mentors have influenced you? How are you a different person because of their influence?

2. What books have you found to be life-changing? Why were they effective?

3. How significant is the tool of prayer in the life of a believer and specifically in your life?

4. What is the importance of identifying your own gifts? If you have done that, what assisted you in the process?

5. If life is a marathon, what have been some of the most trying parts of the race for you? What is the ultimate goal?

THE GOOD NEWS OF JESUS CHRIST

G OD'S LOVE FOR you is the starting point for the message of God's rescue as disclosed in the Bible. The story of His love begins with His creation of man and woman, and placing them in the Garden of Eden. The Bible says, "God blessed them," (Genesis 1:22) demonstrating His love and His desire for them to have His very best. God's attitude is the same toward you. He loves you and desires to bless you with the greatest thing you could ever experience—a close relationship with Himself. You may ask, "If God loves me how do you explain the setbacks and pain I experience?" Often God uses the circumstances of life to bring us to the best—closer to Himself.

Though God loves us and seeks fellowship with us, man's response is rebellion against Him. Rebellion against God's person and standard of righteousness is called sin. It is not just notorious sinners who have failed; the Bible says we all have sinned (Romans 3:23). The greatest effect of sin is that it breaks our relationship with God. He has not turned away from us. We have turned away from Him.

How can man restore his friendship with God? It cannot be done by good works, attempting to earn our forgiveness. We must find a payment for sin, because it is our sin that has violated God's law. In His love and mercy, God has paid the price Himself through His Son Jesus Christ.

Imagine for a moment that you stand before a judge's bench, accused of a crime deserving the death penalty. The judge renders the verdict: "Guilty as charged on all counts. You are condemned to die!" While you are weeping at the foot of his bench, the judge slowly comes down from his seat, removes his robe, then allows himself to be shackled and led off to execution for your crime. The judge himself has chosen to take your place. That is what Christ did for us. He took our place, paying for our sin, when He died on the cross.

Because of His sacrifice, the sin that creates a wall between God and us has been destroyed. All we need to do is believe on Christ and what He has done for us, turning from our rebellion against Him, and yielding our heart to do His will. He stands at the door of our heart (mind, emotions, and will) and seeks entrance (Revelation 3:20). He offers forgiveness and eternal life—life with him beginning now and lasting through eternity—as He transforms us into His image and likeness. The change He works in us allows us to grow in our greatest privilege and joy—close fellowship with Him.

This is the Gospel, the greatest good news in the history of civilization.

RESOURCES FOR FINDING
YOUR SPIRITUAL GIFTS

RECOMMEND TAKING a comprehensive course on spiritual gifts, but will list here some resources that I view as thorough and accurate.

- *TEAM Ministry Resources* (www.ChurchGrowth.org). They offer a course through local churches called "TEAM MINISTRY, A Guide to Spiritual Gifts and Lay Involvement." I trust their materials, and through their website they offer a free Spiritual Gifts Analysis that you can take online. They call it "the nation's best-selling Spiritual Gifts inventory." The questionnaire contains 108 questions, and you'll be given the results based on your answers. I have taken it perhaps four times, and have always found it helpful and accurate.

- *PLACE* (www.placeministries.org). This is a training course that assesses a number of areas including personality (based on the DISC model), spiritual gifts (based on a sixteen-gift model), abilities, passions, and life experiences. They describe it as a "Bible-based, self-discovery process that connects God's people to meaningful ministry." They also have an online assessment priced at $5.95.

• *S.H.A.P.E.* (www.shapediscovery.com). *Finding and Fulfilling Your Unique Purpose in Life* is a book written by Erik Rees. The acronym stands for Spiritual Gifts, Heart, Abilities, Personality, Experiences. The book offers to ". . . help you discover your unique 'S.H.A.P.E.,' explore it, then apply it in ways that will bring confidence, freedom, clarity, and significance." At the related site www.shaperesources.com they offer the Online Serving Sweet Spot Assessment for $14.95.

Though online assessments are available, I recommend learning together with others. After you assess your giftings, sit down with a mature Christian friend for their insights on what ministries you should pursue based on the information you have gained.

BIBLIOGRAPHY

Adams, Jay E., *The Christian Counselor's Manual* (Grand Rapids, MI: Baker Book House, 1973).

Backus, William Backus and Chapian, Marie, *Telling Yourself the Truth* (Minneapolis, MN: Bethany Fellowship, 1980).

Carson, D. A., *How Long O Lord* (Grand Rapids, MI: Baker Books, 1990).

Dr. Cloud, Henry, *Changes That Heal* (Grand Rapids, MI: Zondervan, 1990).

Collins, Gary R., *Christian Counseling, A Comprehensive Guide*, rev. ed. (Nashville, TN: W Publishing Group, 1988).

Collins, Gary R., *Calm Down* (Ventura, CA: Vision House, 1981).

Hybels, Bill, *Understanding God's Purpose for Your Life: Significance*, (Grand Rapids, MI:Zondervan, 1997). Six-part Bible study.

Hyder, Quentin, O., M.D., *The Christian's Handbook of Psychiatry* (Old Tappan, NJ: Fleming H. Revell Company, 1971).

James, John W. and Friedman, Russell, *The Grief Recovery Handbook*, rev. ed. (New York, N.Y.: HarperCollins Publishers, 1998).

Lutzer, Erwin W., *Failure, The Back Door to Success* (Chicago, IL: Moody Press, 1975).

McDonald, Gordon, *Ordering Your Private World* (Nashville, TN: Nelson Books, 1984).

McDowell, Josh, *Building Your Self-Image* (Wheaton, IL: Living Books, Tyndale House, 1984).

McGee, Robert S., *The Search for Significance* (Nashville, TN: Word Publishing, 1998).

McGrath, Joanna and Alister, *Self Esteem, The Cross and Christian Confidence* (Wheaton, IL: Crossway Books, 1992).

Minirth, Frank B. and Meier, Paul D., *Happiness Is a Choice* (Grand Rapids, MI: Baker Book House, 1978).

Minirth, Frank B., *In Pursuit of Happiness, Choices that Can Change Your Life* (Grand Rapids, MI: Fleming H. Revell, 2004).

Moreland, J. P. and Issler, Klaus, *The Lost Virtue of Happiness* (Colorado Springs, CO: Navpress, 2006).

Narramore, Bruce and Counts, Bill, *Guilt and Freedom* (Santa Ana, CA: Vision House Publishers, 1974).

Peretti, Frank, *The Wounded Spirit*, (Nashville, TN: Word Publishing, 2000).

Pyne, Robert A., *Humanity & Sin,* (Nashville, TN: Word Publishing, 1999).

Seamonds, David, *Healing for Damaged Emotions,* (Wheaton, IL: Victor Books, 1986).

Smith, David W., *The Friendless American Male* (Ventura, CA: Regal Books, 1983).

Solomon, Charles R., *The Ins and Out of Rejection* (Littleton, CO: Heritage House Publications, 1976).

Sproul, R. C., *Pleasing God* (Wheaton, IL: Tyndale House Publishers, 1988).

West, Kari, *Dare to Trust, Dare to Hope Again* (Colorado Springs, CO: Cook Communications Ministries, 2001).

Wright, H. Norman, *Making Peace with Your Past* (Grand Rapids, MI: Fleming H. Revell, 1985).

Breinigsville, PA USA
16 February 2011
255684BV00002B/146/P